YA WANNA LAUGH?

Volume 1

Lucille Rains

PRESS

Ya Wanna Laugh?
Volume 1
by Lucille Rains

Printed in the United States of America

ISBN 9781619045002

www.xulonpress.com

CONTENTS

MUSIC

MISCELLANEOUS STORIES

BATHROOM HUMOR
(Enter At Your Own Risk)

DEDICATION

Ya Wanna Laugh? is dedicated to my Mother from whom I inherited my love of humor and my love of the English language. At any free moment while raising nine children, she could be found at the kitchen table copying words from a mammoth unabridged dictionary. Originally from a small farm village in Europe, she taught herself to read and write English. I have a vivid picture of her asleep at the kitchen table with her head on this huge dictionary and the pen still in her hand.

Whenever my mother got that twinkle in her eye and said, "Ya Wanna Laugh?" you knew that a side-splitting story was coming. Sometimes she'd reminisce about her grandmother who told stories that rivaled Aesop. She told my mother that at one time animals could talk. I asked my mother how come they don't talk now, and she answered, "They were troublemakers, so God took away their talk." She gave an example of a cat that broke up a marriage in her grandmother's village by telling the husband that his young bride was entertaining a man while he was at work. I remember asking, "How do you know it's true," and she would say, "My grandmother would never lie."

Such were the stories passed down through generations in my family. Now it's my turn to ask, "Ya Wanna Laugh?" and pass down the stories of *my* generation.

INTRODUCTION

Whenever something funny happened over the course of my life, I'd write a letter about it and then store a copy in my records. I kept them as a memento of my experiences, but I never thought of myself as a writer. I was a musician all the way, practicing piano many hours a day.

During the college years, I was friends with an artistic student who would do instant sketches, particularly of political figures. I thought of him as a cartoonist. When he finished school and went out into the world to seek his fortune, our friendship continued through letters. It surprised me when he said that I should write, that "You are the only one I know who can really write." He was just being kind, I told myself. When he became a famous writer of several best-sellers, I began to feel differently about his words.

After marriage, all music aspirations ended when I found myself the sole breadwinner of my family. In order to accommodate my children's schedule, I needed to go into my own business. Since I'd been tuning my own piano right along, it was easy to transition into the piano business.

Somewhere along the line, I wrote a letter to the editor, first time ever, and it attracted the attention of the mayor. I ended up being her ghostwriter. At the same time, an editor invited me to write a column in the local paper. It was an extraordinary experience to have public response to my writing. It was at this time that my writing career was launched. However, the piano tuning years were not wasted as they gave me rich experiences to write about.

It surprised me to discover that writing is simply another form of music. Instead of using tones, you use words, but the creative process behind the two is the same. In this sense, I am still the musician when I write.

PIANO TUNING

The Piano Sale

Scene I

It was unusual for anyone to shop for a piano on a Friday night, much less expect to have it delivered and tuned that same night, but this was a special occasion. Istvan (pronounced ISHT-von) was getting married over the weekend and he wanted to surprise his bride. He looked at the beautiful high-polished ebony Kawai console that I had for sale in my home/shop, and in his thick Hungarian accent said "LOO-sil, I like, but must have valnut."

I phoned Mihaly (pronounced MEE-hi, but everyone called him Mickey), a Hungarian piano dealer who handled the same model, to get a walnut one, and he said, "LOO-sil, vie you call so late? My vife she kill me. She say I never take out. Tonight, she invite neighbor. Vee going to eat, drink, enchoy. LOO-sil, bring man to store tomorrow."

"Mickey! The man is standing here with a checkbook in his hand! Tomorrow will be too late!"

Mickey thought about that for about ten seconds, then said, "Fok da neighbor, I doan like, anyway. Come to store in hour."

Scene II

By 9:30 p.m. we were heading north with my Volvo Station Wagon leading Mickey's gigantic box truck, like a mouse leading an elephant. After a forty-

15

five minute drive, we pulled into the supermarket lot where we were to meet Istvan. When Istvan showed up in his Volvo Station Wagon, there was an instant recognition between Istvan and Mickey. It turned out that they were from the same village in Hungary, and though they didn't know each other there, they greeted each other here like long lost brothers. They were so caught up reminiscing about the old country, they forgot I was there. I had to wait till they waded through a few decades of village news before we could get back to the piano delivery. They turned to me, and after a series of stereo LOO-sils, we were finally on our way.

Scene III

Istvan led the procession with Mickey's huge box truck behind him and my wagon trailing. Our caravan was now a gigantic dinosaur, with a small head and a small tail and a mammoth body, creeping slowly along an unlit rural road. Istvan turned left onto a near-invisible dirt road that you'd have to know was there or you wouldn't find it. The trees were so thick, they were breaking on the sides of the box truck.

After parking our Volvos in a barely visible cinder block open garage at the lake clearing, Istvan shouted for Mickey to turn the truck around, and he directed it to the very edge of the water. I could not imagine why.

"Istvan, where on earth is this piano going?"

"Vee go to island."

"Island? How?"

"Vee go on pontoon."

It was pitch black and I could see no boat, but as my eyes began to adjust to the dark, I could see something moving. "You mean that door floating in the water? You're going to put this piano on that door?"

"Doan vorry, LOO-sil, pontoon carry t'ousand pounds."

The two men loaded the piano onto the center of this flimsy floating raft as I watched in horror. Mickey sat at the piano, I sat uneasily on the floor next to the piano, clutching my tool box with sweaty palms, and Istvan was in the rear, operating a putt-putt motor. Istvan's dog, Janos (pronounced YAH-noess), a muscular dog who, surprisingly, had a squeak for a bark, stood bravely at the bow facing the black wall of night before us, like a brave sea captain.

I tried to reassure myself by whispering "a t'ousand pounds, a t'ousand pounds," then I began adding it all up. Let me see, the piano is around 450 lbs, the men, at least 200 lbs each, that's 850 lbs. My tools have to be around 50 lbs, that's 900. And then there's the dog and me. My god! That's over a thousand! That's it! We're definitely going to sink! The men were so busy chatting in Hungarian that they never heard my protests. There was nothing I could do but resign myself to certain death. Well, I figured that if I have to go down to the bottom of the lake, at least it's with a Kawai.

While you couldn't see two feet in front of you on the lake, you could see the stars millions of miles away. The night was brisk and clear and the sky was like a comforting blanket over me, so close it seemed you could reach out and touch a star. The beauty of the heavens, the soothing sound of the water lapping against our slow-moving "ship," and the lulling putt-putt of the motor, transported me to a tranquil place where danger didn't exist. It no longer mattered that I didn't know how to swim.

My reverie was soon shattered when Mickey decided to play a Hungarian love song on the piano, flowery arpeggios up and down the keyboard. Specks of light began to come on around the lake. People were no doubt wondering how there could possibly be piano music coming from the center of the lake at almost midnight. It gave me some comfort to know that there were people awake who could hear my cries when we sank.

Scene IV

Our raft bumped to a stop and Istvan announced "Vee here." I could see nothing but the black night around me. You had to look way up to see the faint outline of a cabin atop a mountain, silhouetted against the stars.

"Istvan, are there any lights?" I asked.

"No, no electricity. Vee have chenerator."

It was too dark to see anything, but I could hear Mickey and Istvan hoisting the piano onto a platform. The dog jumped onto it with them, and they all chug-chugged up the side of the mountain. They were so engrossed in chatting about the old country that they never heard my cry, "Hey! What about me?"

I had to get up to the cabin somehow, but I was afraid to touch the rail on which the platform traveled. What if it had juice, like a third rail you read about? My only alternative was to simply crawl up the side of the mountain. It wouldn't have been so bad had I been able to use both hands, but I was carrying a heavy tool case. There were bushes along the way for me to grab hold of and pull myself up while crawling on my knees up the steep incline. By the time I reached the cabin door, I looked like I'd been hit by a freight train and all Istvan could say was, "LOO-sil, vere you go?" Where did he think? Where they left me!

Scene V

The entire cabin was lit by one solitary generator-powered 25 watt bulb that cast shadows everywhere. Dim as it was, there was enough light to see that Istvan's bride-to-be was very pregnant and, in fact, she was in labor.

I said, "Katalin, is it wise for you to be on this island where you have no phone and no electricity?"

Istvan heard me and piped up, "Doan vorry, LOO-sil, doctor coming to vedding."

Oh, how nice, I thought, and what is *he* going to do in an emergency on an island with no electricity?

I tuned the piano by flashlight while Istvan, Mickey, and a few relatives from out-of-state that emerged from the shadows, were drinking and celebrating this triple event: a piano, a birth, and a marriage, possibly in that order. Katalin wisely excused herself and trudged slowly up the stairs to bed. She wasn't particularly interested in partying in her condition. By the time I finished tuning, they were all drunk and laughing loudly at anything and everything.

Then Istvan said to me, "LOO-sil, vee toast piano. C'mon, vee drink togadder."

"No, Istvan, I don't drink. It's late. I have to get home."

Istvan ignored my protests and stuck a glass in my hand.

"What is this, Istvan?"

"Wodka. Vee make toast to piano."

His partying relatives staggered over to us with drinks in their hands and formed a disjointed circle. Istvan shouted a loud Hungarian toast in the air, and everyone threw their head back and inhaled their drink in one gulp. It was dark enough for them not to see—and I'm not so sure any one of them could see straight even if it were light—that I threw my head back with the rest of them and tossed the drink over my right shoulder. When I did that, I heard a protesting squeak by my feet. I didn't know the dog was lying down behind me; and he wouldn't move away, either. Five squeaks later, Istvan was so delighted that I was such a good sport about drinking, he allowed me to leave. I didn't see Mickey anywhere, but I couldn't worry about him. I had to get home.

Istvan said, "I help you," and offered me his unsteady arm in the black outdoors. I expected to take the platform down the mountainside to the pontoon, but instead, we were headed in a different direction. Istvan was so drunk that while he was walking safely on a narrow path, pontificating loudly about the universe like a dramatic orator, with left arm sweeping broadly across the vast expanse of starlit sky, he left no room for me and led me into every possible hole and rock on the side of the path. At one point, Istvan was so preoccupied with his philosophical babbling, now accompanied by deep hiccupping, that he failed to notice that I had fallen to my knees in a hole. He just kept talking and walking, dragging me out of the hole without missing a step, his left arm still waving dramatically.

It suddenly struck me that I had to rely on this inebriated man to bring me safely across the lake to my car, a man who could hardly utter a single rational, undistorted word, nor take one firm step. I asked Istvan, with fearful recollection, "Are we going back on the pontoon?"

His happy reply was, "No, vee go by spidboat."

"Spidboat! Oh my god!"

Scene VI

His speedboat was moored at a floating pier. It took several stumbles before he could plop me, then himself, successfully into the boat. It took even more uncoordinated tries to get the key into the ignition. When he finally started up the motor, he gave it so much gas that the front of the boat bolted upright and we skipped across the surface of the lake in vertical position, like astronauts headed toward the moon. This ride made the pontoon ride seem like a pleasure cruise.

Istvan had made this trip so many times that he didn't need his mind. The boat knew the way. As we neared the pier at the clearing, he managed to turn off the motor after a few tries. When we hit, he stood up and stuck one unsteady foot out of the boat onto the pier. He was trying to tie the boat to a post but he kept missing. The boat started to drift away from the pier, and Istvan's legs slowly parted until he was in a full split. While hovering precariously over the water, he somehow managed to inch the boat and the pier together, finally securing the boat. It was like watching a Charlie Chaplin movie.

Istvan leaned over the edge of the pier to help me out of the boat, but with so little coordination, he misjudged, and yanked me up so fast that my head hit his chin and his head snapped back, almost knocking him out. As he reeled backwards, I remember thinking, "If this guy falls off the pier, he's just going to have to die, because I can't save him. It's too dark, and I can't swim.

He did some fancy Fred Astaire footwork, tee-tering on the very edge of the pier a few times. I didn't wait around for him to recover his balance, but ran toward the faint outline of my car in the cinder block garage. I fumbled for my keys, then nervously started up. I quickly backed out and as I was taking off, Istvan unexpectedly stuck his head in the window. In my frenzy, I drove off with his head. He hung on as long as he could, still babbling incoherently about the stars or the universe or something, and then dropped off with a dull thud. I could hear a cheerful "Goodnight, LOO-sil" from the ground, so I knew he was still alive, and I drove home like I had just escaped prison.

Some piano sales are just a little more difficult than others.

Death By Spinet

When I go from tuning a Steinway Grand to an old beat-up spinet, I get the aural bends. While I'm in this frame of mind, people should *never* make the mistake of asking what I think of these little mutants because I am no longer tactful. I don't care at all how emotionally attached a person is to grandma's spinet, that piano belongs at the curb, piece by piece if necessary. If grandma is still alive and objects, put her at the curb, too. It's all her fault.

Sometimes, as I am standing before a little beast and am asked "Can you fix this piano?" I have been known to answer "Do you believe in miracles?" Once I was so overwhelmed by the weird sounds coming out of the guts of the spinet, I said, "This piano doesn't need a tuner, it needs an exorcist." I was so absolutely appalled at the state of a woman's spinet that when she asked "Can this piano be saved" I remember answering, "Only if it can repeat the Sinner's Prayer." Press me to rate an old, beat-up spinet from one to ten, I'm likely to say "Minus 2." When it comes to these spinets, people imagine that you can make a silk purse out of a sow's ear, but it can't be done. IT'S A SOW'S EAR, PEOPLE, AND WILL REMAIN A SOW'S EAR NO MATTER WHAT YOU DO! The only use for these old beat-up pianos is target practice.

A psychotherapist asked me what I thought of his spinet after wrestling with the ogre for several hours. I answered, "One more piano like yours and I'll end up on your couch."

One time I opened up the top of a spinet that was a minor third down in pitch and so horrendous in all ways, it no longer qualified as a musical instrument. It had a split right across the pin block. I remember saying, "Whoever took an axe to this piano had the right idea."

People's piano vocabulary never ceases to amaze me. In one old spinet whose plastic elbows were shattering thus preventing the hammers from playing, the lady said, "My knockers don't work." I answered, "Sorry to hear that, but let's talk about the piano."

I will never understand how these people keep having me back. In fact, a spinet-owner whose jack springs were breaking one by one, asked me to tune her piano recently but, mercifully, my car was in the shop. She offered to pay round trip for a cab. I told her that I had a broken leg. Then she told me that she's giving grandma's old spinet to her daughter so the grandkids can take lessons. Here we go again with that grandma thing. If she knows how bad the piano is, why would she give it to family just because it was grandma's? I told the woman to give that spinet to someone she hates.

Even a new spinet can be a tinny monstrosity. A client of mine, Les Paul, that legend who invented multi-track recording and the solid body electric guitar that launched the whole rock movement, once told me, proudly, "Baldwin is putting out a Les Paul spinet."

I looked at him in horror and said, "And you're letting them?" He was shaken by my response and quickly said, "Well, maybe it's a console." Yeah, right.

I instructed my daughter that when I die, please inscribe across the top of my headstone, Death By Spinet, because that will undoubtedly be the cause.

The Perfect Piano Job

I did a piano job for a young doctor who surprised me with one of the most sensitive statements I've ever heard about something that I love deeply. He said that music was the very breath of God. I've always felt this way but have never heard anyone else express it, least of all a doctor. But he was unique. As successful as his medical practice was, he felt that music was his true profession. But then, this doctor was such a creative genius, he could have gone into any field. There wasn't anything he could not do, and do well. He re-upholstered his own antique pieces; wrote prose and poetry; played several instruments; did all of his own landscaping that made his property look like a manicured park. He also knew all about nutrition and was a gourmet cook and, if all of that wasn't enough, he was into physical fitness with his daily early morning brisk walks and exercise. His healthful life was reflected in his clear complexion, sparkling eyes, and boundless energy.

The only blemish in this picture-perfect life was the doctor's piano. In good faith, he bought a 6-ft grand from a friend who loved it so much, he wanted someone he knew to have it so he could have access to it. The doctor misunderstood his friend's enthusiasm and assumed that this piano was a treasure. He was so caught up in his friends enthusiasm, he paid double what the piano was worth. After the piano was moved to Doc's house and he had a chance to live with it, he was very disappointed, and rightfully so. It had a tone like alley cats caterwauling on the back fence and an action as creaky as the stairs in a condemncd house.

It was time to transform this piano, so I had Doc help me carry the piano action to a nearby table and thought he would go away and let me work, but he wouldn't leave. He was like an anxious parent who insisted on staying in the hospital all night with a sick child. There was no way I could get him out of the room, so I did the next best thing and put him to work. I gave him an assignment to clean the inside of the piano now that the guts were out of it, and I showed him what to do. He was delighted to be a part of this 'operation.'

His medical training must have kicked in because before he would touch the piano, he scrubbed up and put on a pair of rubber gloves. He brought in an industrial size box of surgical gauze, Q-tips, forceps, and of course, he boiled water. What good is an operation if you don't boil water? As he was cleaning the piano bed, he was telling me that he always wanted a Baby Grand. He repeated it so many times, I half wondered if he thought he was going to deliver one the way he was reaching into the open front of the piano with his sterile gloved hands.

I watched him out of the corner of my eye. He cleaned the soundboard with the surgical gauze and disposed of it with the forceps. He used a whole box of Q-Tips to clean the hard-to-get-at area under the strings around the tuning pins, all of this in addition to the usual vacuuming. I doubt that any piano in existence has ever had such a clinical cleaning as this one.

When he finished, he disinfected himself—I could smell it—then I heard him bustling about in the kitchen. In short time, the magnificent aroma of gourmet cooking filled the air. I could hardly concentrate on my work.

Finally, we put the action back into the piano, I tuned it, and then I sat down to play. I always do that to check my work. Suddenly, Doc came rushing into the room with a black case, opened it quickly, pulled out a trumpet and joined right in. We played old standards for at least a half hour. He was great! Maybe he was right. Maybe music was his true profession.

He was so ecstatic over the piano transformation, he insisted on sharing the gourmet food that he prepared. Nice as the doc was, I have watched enough Forensic Files to make sure that both plates were filled from the same pot and that he took the first bite—I'm not that stupid—then I dug in.

This superb meal was the perfect ending to a perfect piano job.

A Tuner's Travels

A tuner never knows what country he/she will be visiting each day. Take the following day, for example.

I was commissioned to not only tune a piano for a book publishing party to celebrate the 'poi-try'—as they called it—of two writers, but also to provide the music for it. The other musician and I played both bass and piano, so we surprised the 'poi-ets' by switching instruments from time to time. It surprised and pleased them.

The writers were my friend, Juanita, and her Armenian colleague who represented a writers' organization called "The Word Shoppe." After the cocktail hour, there were two separate tables of food, Armenian and American. I dove for the Armenian table with its chopped-pecan-filled Baklava. It was excellent! And the punch! It had huge strawberries floating in it. Good thing I got my four glasses in quickly because it was gone in minutes.

After this gig, I had an appointment to meet this short middle-age guy named Vito to look at a free piano for him. I can't imagine what this man wanted with a piano. Maybe he had grandchildren—I don't know, but that was none of my business. My job was to examine the piano to see if it was worth taking. I'm always suspicious of a free piano. It usually means that the owner would rather give it away than pay the exorbitant dumping costs.

We had to go look at the piano in his huge Mac truck because my acoustic bass fiddle took up the whole back of my Volvo Wagon with the neck protruding into the passenger seat, so there was no room for him. The step into his truck was so high, I had to climb up on my knees and reach for the hand grips to pull myself up. I was concerned about leaving my car on the street with my bass in it, but Vito assured me that "Nobody a-steal here. I leave-a my truck open all-a time." All I could think was, it may be easier to sell a Czech Bass on the street than a Mac truck.

The piano was another one of those spinets that I warn people about. It had a badly cracked sound board, broken elbows, and was a third below pitch, perfect for target practice. I gave my professional advice to Vito, "Tell these people to give the piano to an enemy." Then we went back to Vito's house. I was relieved to see that nobody a-steal my bass.

But before I left, he showed me his still. He openly admitted that the building for the still was illegal but that he had friends and relatives all around, and "nobody a-squeal." If what I was sensing about this man were true, no one would dare a-squeal.

He was also proud of his homemade wine, and he pressed two bottles into my arms, "one a-red and one a-white." He never heard me say that I don't drink. I suppose I could use one of them to christen my son's new pontoon.

The guy had a commercial pizza oven on his patio instead of a grill, and he gave pizza parties for the whole neighborhood. He even invited me to one.

Then he waved his hand toward his manicured land and proudly announced, "You see my pitches?"

"Pitches?" I looked around. I wasn't sure what I was supposed to see. I didn't see any baseball players around.

He pointed to some trees and said, "Pitches, pitches."

I studied the trees and finally saw what he was talking about. "Oh, I see. You have peaches. That's very nice, Vito." Then I made a beeline to my car.

After a tuning, a gig, and an appraisal, I was tired. It had been a rich, full day, but it was time to return to my own country.

Tuning Out Mr. Polfuss

A man with a name that sounded like Polfuss called for a piano tuning. He lived in a private community that could only be reached by crossing a narrow bridge over a river. His home appeared to be anchored on a mountainside with rock blasted away for parking. As I pulled up in the back, an elderly gentleman with piercing blue eyes, wild wiry white hair, and one arm in a sling came out to greet me. This was already unusual, as people seldom go out of their way to greet the piano tuner. We're lucky if they answer the door.

I followed him through a side entrance of an addition that may have been a garage at one time. He turned right and led me along a corridor to a thick door that looked like it belonged on a bank vault. The corridor had no furnishings except for a long counter that you might see in a department store, but there was nothing in or on it other than a phone. This was a far cry from the standard tuning job where the piano is in the living room.

I was somewhat apprehensive about stepping through that ominous door into a pitch black room. Right about here, my years of watching *The Twilight Zone* kicked in. Was I about to enter another time period? Was this man a mad scientist who needed one more person on the space ship? Did he really have a piano?

He disappeared and I stood silently in the dark until a few lights came on. The lights were so high, they looked like stars and did not cast much light. What they did was to cast shadows that made the room look sinister. As my eyes adjusted to the dark, I began to make out forms strewn about the large windowless room. In the center was the biggest form of all. Flashlight in hand, I discovered that it was a Steinway B grand piano, one of the finest I have ever played. Astonished, I turned to him and said, "Gee Mr. Polfuss, you really *do* take your music seriously, don't you?"

While I was inspecting the piano by flashlight, he disappeared once more to put some lights on in what was obviously a control room. Imagine, I thought, this old coot had his own recording studio right in his home. I was impressed. I figured that he must be an eccentric old millionaire with a passion for music.

As I tuned, Mr. Polfuss stood nearby and carried on a nostalgic soliloquy about the good old days. He dropped so many famous names, I figured the man was delusional from watching too many old black and white movies, or that he was in the early stages of something or other. At one point, he mentioned that his house was used to televise *The Ozzie and Harriet Show*. Yeah, and I'm Cleopatra.

It was a struggle to tune while Mr. Polfuss continued this biographical drone about the famous people he knew, like Bing Crosby and Judy Garland. By the time he got to Claudette Colbert, I'd had enough. I put my tuning hammer down and said, "This is all very interesting, Mr. Polfuss, but would you please go into the other room so I can tune this piano?"

Somewhat startled, he stopped talking, looked at me for a moment, and then left the room. The rest of the job was uneventful.

On my drive home, I got to thinking about this old man. There was something familiar about that face. Remembering that in his stories he was called "Red" by all the famous people he mentioned, I tried to visualize Mr. Polfuss with red hair. Then it dawned on me. I know who this man is. He is the music legend Les Paul, the guitarist who invented the multi-track recording and the solid body electric guitar. This is the man who single-handedly launched the Rock Movement—much to many people's chagrin (including mine, speaking as the mother of a rock musician).

I really didn't expect to hear from him after kicking him out of his own studio, but he did call again. The sling was gone and he was once again a recognizable redhead. Once I knew who he was, though, it was OK if he talked a lot and stuck his head in the piano with mine. As a genius inventor, he is compelled to see how things work. In fact, I let him help me fix a broken part on his magnificent Steinway B.

By 90, Les Paul wore hearing aids on both ears. He says that someone came up behind him, slapped their hands over his ears and said, "Guess who?" Les says that this sudden smack broke both ear drums and led to a hearing problem. When his hearing aid proved to be unsatisfactory, he redesigned it and patented it. It makes sense. Hearing aids, like electric guitars, deal with sound amplification.

Les Paul's recording studio sports a picture of his mother, whom he said lived to be 103. If he carries the same genes, he will probably meet that figure. At 90, he's still going strong. He still drives, still gigs every Monday in New York City, still records, is still inventing, and has a lively spring in his step.

But I kind of wish he hadn't told me that a guitar company is putting out a "Les Paul" spinet. There are enough problems in life.

Moe

It was Christmastime and I got a call to work on a beat-up grand piano that any reputable piano technician would have advised putting at the curb. But Moe, short for Mohammed, a 50ish man with one white pony tail down his back and a thick Iranian accent, is eking out a living teaching piano on it, so it had to be salvaged at any cost. Correction: It had to be salvaged at NO cost. Moe was poor.

Moe wasn't old enough to live in a retirement village, but it was the only affordable place he could find. All I saw in this huge apartment complex were elderly widows, and they treated Moe like the building mascot. He helped them with repairs (God help them, he's clumsy) and they reciprocated by driving him to the store. He has no car; too costly.

Standing at his door automatically set off a motion-sensor Santa who let out a loud Ho-Ho-Ho that scared me half to death. Since he shared an entry with other people, that Ho-Ho-Ho was triggered at least every fifteen minutes. If only I had brought a baseball bat!

When I stepped into his apartment, I was hit in the face with a blast of heat that singed my eyebrows, so I asked, "Why do you keep your place so hot, Moe? Is it because you're used to the hot climate in Iran?"

"No, no. In Iran, I go skiing."

"Skiing?"

"Yes, we climb up mountain and we ski."

Well, at least I learned something about Iran. Then he politely turned down the heat.

His condo was decorated for teaching piano to children, so when you step in, you enter a Wonderland. Everywhere you looked, it was Porky Pig or Goofy or talking animals, and I mean everywhere: the rugs, pictures on the walls, on every piece of furniture, smiley faces on the backs of chair covers, the bathroom shower curtain, everywhere. It makes you want to burst into "It's A Small World After All." Two huge stuffed German Shepherds startled me, they were so lifelike! There were vats of candy and prizes and, in fact, he filled a bag for me when I left.

His bedroom was set up as a waiting room for parents, so there were wall-to-wall dolls, games, and toys for siblings. I don't think he missed one single Disneyland animal. I remember thinking, "Am I in the gingerbread house?"

And everything was neurotically spotless. Moe was a perfectionist, worse than Felix Unger on Odd Couple.

Moe liked to "fix" things, especially things he knew nothing about, including the piano. He broke around eight hammers pulling the action out of the piano before I arrived. He said that the keys were too bouncy, so he tried turning this screw and that screw. Moe's fearless adjustments made the piano unplayable. Additionally, he didn't want to disturb his neighbors with his playing, so he glued little pieces of rubberized felt on the tip of each hammer. This made the keys that worked sound like it was two miles away.

He sat by me as I worked. I'd use a tool, then another, and when I reached for the first tool again, he had already put it away. I had to say, "Moe, don't touch the tools!" He'd just grin like a mischievous child but nothing would change. So I decided to put him to work. I'd say, "OK, Moe, get me the first tool again," and he was as happy as a clam being my assistant. I even gave him little jobs to do, but I had to watch him. He's totally fearless and recklessly rushes in where angels fear to tread, usually breaking something.

His suggestions showed me why his piano was in such disrepair. I glued something, and he said, "Do you want me to get my hair dryer to dry the glue?"

"No, Moe, heat softens glue. Leave it alone."

With all the tools I brought, I didn't have any graphite. He wanted to use the lubricant that he uses on his shaver.

"No, Moe, we don't use shaver lubricant on pianos."

"But it's good."

"I know, Moe, but no, Moe."

Thoroughly immersed in this pitiful piano, I said "Moe, bring me some alcohol."

So what does Moe do? He brings me a bottle of wine.

So I said, "No, Moe, this is not a party. I need rubbing alcohol to un-stick this piece."

So he says, "No alcohol, no alcohol." Then he's thinking, and says, "Wait, I get."

He comes back with a bottle of wine vinegar.

I looked at him, I looked at the wine vinegar, and I thought, Oh well, the piano's shot anyway. I was getting light-headed from hunger, so without expending another ounce of caution, I went along with it. I put wine vinegar on the part, and guess what? It worked.

Since I was doing the work gratis, Moe was preparing a beautiful dinner for me. If nothing else, the man can cook. The delightful aroma of roasting chicken was making my head spin. Since the table had the piano action on it, he had me sit on the couch to eat.

First, he brings out this beautiful chicken made to perfection in a George Foreman oven, and he puts it on an end table for me to look at in painful anticipation. When he left to get a chair to use as a table for me, I had all to do to keep from grabbing the chicken and running with it under my arm like a football player running toward the goal post, but I wasn't about to leave my tools there, so I sat there and salivated.

He then lifts a chair to set before me as a table, and he's talking so much, he doesn't realize that he stuck one chair leg through the chicken. He never noticed, and I never said anything. I was so hungry I was going to eat that chicken no matter what.

Then he asked, "Do you want blue cheese or oil & vinegar on your salad?" I chose blue cheese, so he goes into the kitchen and brings me this strange orange dressing with Paul Newman's picture on it; I think it was Thousand Island.

"Moe, where is the blue cheese?"

He looks at the bottle and says, "This is NOT blue cheese?"

"No, Moe. It's *not* blue cheese, but that's OK, I'll use it anyway."

Then he was happy. He was so childlike, I wondered if his kindergarten environment was for himself.

While I was eating, he decided to entertain me with a classical CD of a French soprano who screamed with all her might throughout the disk, scaling up and down three octaves. It made me seasick.

He said, proudly, "You see, she doesn't use words."

I said, "Well neither does a French soprano who is being mugged. Turn it off, OK?"

When I left, the piano wasn't great, but at least it worked enough to teach on—IF he could teach. I never heard him play. Actually, he could be a musical genius for all I know.

Last I heard, Moe was banned from teaching piano in his condo. He never read the association rules that prohibited running a business on the premises, so unless he got a special dispensation from the association committee, all my work was in vain.

Oh, well, at least I got a chicken dinner and a bag of candy. What more can you ask?

The Nursing Home Piano

The nursing home piano was in a large multi-purpose room that is not only equipped as a dining hall, but has a TV area and little make-shift classrooms around the edge of the room. The piano was near the TV, which was on. When the aide was asked to turn it off so I could tune, she swung all the wheelchairs around so the occupants could watch the tuning. So now the tuning replaced the TV as an activity. I didn't mind this white-haired, distracted audience, except that one woman barked louder than the piano so that I had to tune in between barks.

A Yugoslavian music teacher had set up her little keyboard in the far corner of the room and began teaching her group old American favorites, like *On Top Of Old Smokey*. You have not lived until you've heard *On Top Of Old Smokey* sung with a thick Yugoslavian accent.

The last time I did this piano, there was a cooking class going on. This is hard to understand since the occupants are in wheelchairs and there is no stove. But who am I to question? The piano had to be pushed into the hall for the tuning so that it would not interfere with the cooking class.

One latecomer came rolling at top speed down the hall and parked in front of me. She watched the tuning with intense concentration, then said, "When you finish, can I taste it?" "Of course," I answered, after doing a double-take. Who am I to refuse a kindly senior a taste of my seasoned tuning? At least she wasn't like the old gentleman who leaned over the piano and said, "When are you gonna finish? You gimme a headache," or a patient with a black wig like a nest atop her white hair who said, "Hurry up with the piano, I hafta get home!"

Oh, well. At least nobody shot at me.

Pass The Cheese, Please

Roger Baldwin was that spry nonagenarian who lived in the Thomas Kinkade-like cottage on the most breathtakingly beautiful pond I had ever seen. I was sure that the scenic view through the music room French doors that overlooked the trees and colorful flowers reflected in the still water, all were the source of his good health and boundless energy. I remember thinking, "If everyone had a view like this, there would be no more sickness in the world."

When I first received the call from Mr. Baldwin, I had no idea that he was the founder of the American Civil Liberties Union (ACLU). That day, my earlier piano job ran into a snag and I was running late. When I told Mr. Baldwin that I had had no time for lunch, he asked if I would like some cheese and crackers. I readily accepted. Meanwhile, I opened up the piano and began tuning while waiting for him to return with the food. I waited, and I waited, but it was not forthcoming. The hunger pangs were getting stronger and by now, my hypoglycemia was kicking in, making me lightheaded and weak. I put down my tuning hammer and went looking for Mr. Baldwin.

He was in the living room flanked by a group of very important-looking well-dressed people. Their deep discussion abruptly ceased when I entered the room, and all heads turned towards me—no doubt wondering what the emergency was. After all, what reason would a person have to interrupt a Baldwin meeting short of a national emergency or a call from the president of the United States? They sat silently, awaiting my urgent message. Then I spoke.

"Mr. Baldwin, where is the cheese you promised me?"

Their stunned faces turned toward Mr. Baldwin like the audience at a tennis match, wondering what his reaction would be to so frivolous a request.

He looked puzzled, then suddenly remembered. "Oh, I'm so sorry." He jumped up, excused himself, walked briskly toward the kitchen, and returned with the cheese and crackers. I thanked him profusely and left them to their meeting. They sank right back into their deep discussion, no doubt choosing to forget my intrusion.

I ate my treasured booty by the French doors so that I could absorb spiritual strength from the view while regaining physical strength from the food. Once restored, I was able to tackle the huge old ornate Knabe upright that was very much like Roger N. Baldwin, himself. It had character and strength, and was built to last a century.

Sylvia

I was in the hospital for eight days with salmonella poisoning, and was unable to work for some time afterwards. Most of my customers understood, but one woman, a singer/pianist, was persistent. She kept calling me up, saying "Well, when are you going to start tuning again?" Then one day she called and bellowed, "Lucille, puhleeeeze . . . you've got to come and tune my piano."

"Sylvia, I'm really not ready to go back to work, yet. I'm still very weak." I hated to refuse, but what could I do?

"Lucille, you've got to help me out. I've used two tuners since you were here last and one was worse than the other. I can't go on like this. I don't even feel like playing piano anymore." I figured she must be exaggerating, but there was no stopping her. "If I hadn't paid them cash, I would have stopped payment, but I didn't discover how bad they were until they were out the door."

Overwhelmed at the thought of a tuning in my condition, I scrambled for excuses. "Sylvia, I can't drive."

"That's OK, I'll pick you up."

"But I can't even lift my tool bag." "Don't worry about it. I'll carry it." "Sylvia, I can't stand up for long periods."

"There's a couch in the room. You can lie down whenever you want, and take as long as you like. Take all day, if you need to."

Nothing was getting through to her and I was running out of excuses. Then, out of the blue, she says, "What do you like to eat? What is your favorite food?"

I walked right into that one. "I love a good homemade chicken dinner."

So she says, "You got it! I'm making you the best chicken dinner you ever had, with mashed potatoes and string beans and homemade apple pie for dessert . . ."

With no more excuses left, I was about to issue a flat "No" when she added, ". . . and I'll pay you triple."

I thought about that for about ten seconds, then with sudden renewed vigor, I answered, "What time will you be picking me up, Sylvia?"

The Wake

A respected tuner well into his nineties collapsed onstage while tuning a Bechstein Grand that was rented for a concert that night. One of the greatest features about tuning is that there is no retirement cut-off age. If you're a decent tuner, you can work till your last breath, which is obviously what this fine tuner did. The news spread among his fellow technicians and we all sadly resolved to meet at the funeral parlor a few days later.

The night of the viewing, I had to work late, and sped to the funeral parlor before the closing time of 9:00 PM. It had to be a quarter to nine when I got there and to my dismay, the parking lot was packed. I had no idea he had so many friends and relatives. Between my exhaustion from a full day's work, rushing to get to the funeral parlor and searching for a parking space, my stress level was very high.

I rushed up the stairs, into the foyer, quickly signed the guest register, and entered the viewing room. At the front of the room I could see the white-haired nonagenarian lying there in peaceful repose. The room was packed, but I could see no one I knew. I realized that I was late and my colleagues had to work the next day, so they must have paid their respects earlier then left.

Stranger though I was, I mingled with the crowd, and a friendly group invited me to join them at the relative's house of the deceased where there would be a spread of food. I was all set to go with them, when

I picked up a card that memorialized the deceased. To my horror, it was not the name of my fellow tuner. Not only that, the deceased nonagenarian was a woman.

I ran out of the room and looked up at the name plate, and sure enough, it read Annie something. Annie? I couldn't understand it. I knew I was in the right funeral parlor. Bewildered, I looked across the long hall, and there was another wake going on. No wonder the parking lot was full; there were two wakes going on. I ran over to that name plate, and there it was, the room where I was supposed to be. What are the chances of there being a wake for two nonagenarians at the same place and at the same hour, nonagenarians who, by that age, look alike?

I signed the register, second one that night, and entered the room. When my fellow tuners came up to me, I breathed a sigh of relief. I was finally in the right place.

On the way home, I couldn't help but think about my error with some amusement. What must the people at the first wake think about a person who met and shook hands with everyone in the room, accepted an invitation to follow the crowd to a relative's house, then who ended up running down the hall like a crazed animal? And to think that my name is on the register of a stranger's deceased great, great grandmother.

Sometimes I think I'm working too hard.

The Referee

Someone gave this ninety-two year old woman a free piano. I have no idea why she even wanted a piano. She couldn't possibly play with such gnarled arthritic fingers, but that was none of my business. All I know is that people seldom give away a good piano to a stranger. They usually give away a piano to avoid dumping costs, so I don't have to tell you the condition this piano was in. My work was laid out for me.

The elderly woman leaned on her walker as she led me into the living room and then sat on the couch near me. She let me know periodically that her son, the minister, was coming at Noon.

Noon came and left. Then one, and now it was two.

She was agitated when the front door finally opened, and her son stepped in. He greeted her with a cheery "Hello, Mom, how ya doin' today?" but she was miffed.

She wouldn't even look directly at him but turned her eyes down and gave him a cold "You're late!"

"Someone in need came into the office that I had to console," he explained, "but I have the rest of the day, now."

She didn't care about his apology. He was late and there was no acceptable excuse.

"You lied," she said, with great passion and pain.

"You know I don't lie, Mom."

"You could have called."

"I couldn't. Something turned up and I had to take care of it."

By this time, the son gave up trying to reason with her. He now was kneeling before his mother saying, "Forgive me, Mom. Will you please forgive me?"

"You're supposed to be a minister and you would do this to your mother?"

After a few more choruses on his knees, he sat next to her on the couch and cradled her in his arms, and said, softly, "Mom, please forgive me. I'm sorry I'm late, but it was unavoidable."

This saga went on near the piano for at least a half hour with no end in sight. This stony-faced woman just would not relent no matter how penitent her son was. There was no forgiveness for his unpardonable sin.

I got so disgusted, I put my tuning hammer down—it was hopeless to try to tune with this soap opera going on within earshot—and I turned toward them and shouted, "For heavensake, Lady, forgive this damn minister so that I can get on with my work!"

They both looked at me in shock. Actually, I shocked myself, but how long was I expected to wait for this drama to end? If I wanted to go to a play, I would have bought a ticket.

No sooner did I shout my command at these two when the lady turned to her son and said, "I forgive you," and just like that, it was over.

Then they got up and went into the kitchen— probably to get away from me–and I was able to finish this bomb she acquired that resembled a piano.

It was the first time I ever had to be a referee, but I figured it could have been worse. There could have been a parrot in the room screeching throughout the whole job, like another tuner described at our last chapter meeting.

My Colleagues

One night, after a piano technician's chapter meeting, seven of the guys decided to go to Hooters and they invited me to go along. First time ever. The only woman in this chapter, I think they thought of me as their mascot. Of course, on the way into the club, they threatened to put me in a Hooters' outfit and walk in like that. It was the dead of winter, so I asked them, with a straight face, how they thought a sexy Hooter's outfit would look over my thermals?

We walked into a sepia setting and were hit in the face with thunderous music, music that consisted mainly of rumbling bass notes that you could feel in your feet as well as hear. I doubt anyone could recognize the song. It sounded like a helicopter hovering over the room.

With eight of us, we ended up sitting at two tables pushed together, four at a table. The place was so noisy, we couldn't hear past the person next to us. This made conversation difficult, so our conversations fell into two groups of four with two separate conversations going on.

At one table, they were talking about problem pianos, but at my table, we were talking about problem piano owners, especially those who don't believe in paying. The solution to deadbeat piano owners is different in the mind of a man and a woman. Men are more direct.

One guy went to a bar owned by the deadbeat, and held him against the wall by the throat, feet dangling, until he ordered the bartender to slip $1,800 in the tuner's pocket. As I said, men are direct.

Then there's the woman's solution. It only happened to me once. I get to this mansion in an affluent area and the maid lets me in. I tune the piano, and the woman says, "I'll send you a check."

I waited a week, no check, so I called her. "I just put the check in the mail. You should get it on Monday." It never came, so I called again. This time, the maid said, "The Mistress is in Europe." Oh really?

I went to the house just as the maid was carrying groceries in. I even helped her. Then I told her I had to finish the piano. I went up to the piano and unwound as many tuning pins as I could within very short time, and the piano was rendered unplayable. In other words, I TOOK BACK MY TUNING. I thanked the maid and left. Their next call to me wasn't pretty, but I think they got the message. Hopefully, they paid the next tuner.

After the group drank enough beers, it was time to tell jokes. One said, B-Flat, D-Flat and F went into a bar and ordered drinks. The bartender told D-Flat "We don't serve minors here," so D-Flat had to leave. After that, B-Flat and F shared a fifth together." (If you don't know music, you'll never understand this joke. Hint: Bb to Db is a minor 3rd. Bb to F is a perfect fifth.)

I told them a funny story about my late husband. He was on staff at CBS and got a call from a contractor for a gig on bass trombone. My husband said, "But I don't play bass trombone. I don't even have a bass trombone." The contractor said, "I'll rent one for you." My husband said, "You might as well rent an alto sax while you're at it. I don't play that either."

Anyway, despite the noise, the deafening music, and the shouting, we had a great time at Hooters. I even had an inch of beer out of curiosity. Frankly, it tasted like poison. One guy kept saying, "You have to have food with it," so when my food came, I sipped it with my food, and it made the food taste like poison. Drinking is just not for me. The last time I tried to drink, it was a daiquiri. I had to rush outside the club and puke. There were people out there, and when they heard all these deep puking sounds, they all began to applaud. Only in New York! It *was* ridiculous and I tried to laugh, but it's not easy to laugh and puke at the same time.

My invitation to Hooters with the guys was not merely a little informal tête-à-tête, it was an acceptance of a woman as an equal into what had been for many years, a man's field.

FRIENDS AND ACQUAINTANCES

College Daze

One time a college friend and I boarded a bus and suddenly he dropped down in the aisle and had what appeared to be a grand mal seizure, with torso convulsing, eyeballs rolling up into his head, and loud guttural sounds deep in his throat. I stood there dumbfounded. I never knew he had epilepsy. The passengers were horrified. The bus didn't move. Suddenly he sprung up, brushed himself off, and strutted to the back of the bus as though nothing had happened. He looked at me with that twinkle in his eye, so I knew it was just T.K. being T.K. (That's what he preferred to be called.)

I wanted to laugh, but with all those rattled people on the bus turning to see if he was all right, I had to continue the pretense of a worried friend. My laughter didn't explode till we got off the bus and the door slammed shut behind us.

Another time, we ended up in front of an art shop studying the ornate Medieval lettering of the sign that read, YE OLDE ART SHOPPE. Without saying a word, eyes focused on the sign, T.K. fished around in his book bag and pulled out a piece of chalk. I never asked T.K. what he was going to do because he was always up to something. I simply expected the bizarre, and was never disappointed.

In equally fancy script, artist that he was, he put an "F" in front of Art. Then, with smug satisfaction, he stood back to admire his artistic ability and wit. I didn't laugh, but studied it soberly. Then, in a slow-motion gesture, eyes fixed on the sign, mimicking T.K.'s artistic thrust, I took the chalk from his hand and put a "C" in front of Olde. His wit and talent having been challenged and equaled, we strutted away proudly, like two people who had really contributed something worthwhile to the world.

Restaurants offered a wonderful springboard for T.K.'s occasional ribald humor. It was during these quiet repasts that he fed me tidbits of wisdom. "If you ever cut your finger, Luce, never put it in your mouth. The mouth is full of germs. You'd be safer sticking it up your butt." (He was so romantic!) He also told me what a 2-point freep was, but I won't go into that here. When he'd tell me these vital facts of life, I'd listen intently, study his face, then say, "So, T.K., what else are they teaching you over at Yale?"

One time while we were having lunch in a restaurant, he said, "Y'know, Luce, waitresses don't listen to a thing you say." He set out to prove it to me. When the busy waitress rushed over and asked quickly, "How's everything?" T.K. smiled, nodded, and said, politely, "Rat's ass." The waitress nodded back and answered, "Thank you!" and rushed over to another table. That one sent the tea out of my nose.

There were times when T.K. would pound his chest and make jungle sounds. I think he was trying to conjure up a primitive side, but I was never convinced he had one. He was too educated, too polite, spoke in a soft velvety southern accent, and his hands were much too smooth. Of course, it didn't help that he had taken ballet and walked a little too gracefully.

Nonetheless, the American people apparently loved his antics as he went on to become famous.

Leave Me A-Lawn

My landscaper friend and I happened to meet one day in the supermarket. His cart contained a mountain of baby food. He must have aged ten years since I saw him a few months earlier and he acted like he was sleepwalking.

He explained, "I went to a meeting last night and the first thing someone asked me, as I was staggering about with half-closed eyes, was, 'When was the last time you slept? You look terrible!'"

"My mind was so foggy, I couldn't remember. There is no such thing as a full night sleep in my house. I have a 9 year old, a 5 year old, and 3 year old twins, and we only have a two-bedroom house, so all the children sleep in one bedroom. If one wakes up, they *all* wake up, and it's bedlam. Also, if one gets sick, they *all* get sick; but no matter what, I have to get up and go to work the next day. I don't know if I'll ever get through this period alive."

It was not surprising that shoppers walked by us quickly and warily. My friend's brow was furrowed and he spoke with arms flailing about. He was so distraught, I ignored the other customers' unspoken disdain and let the poor man rave on to his weary heart's content.

"Do you know what my worst enemy is?" he asked, with a crazed look on his face, and no intention of letting me guess, "The crayon. That innocent-looking little implement that is placed in the hands of children. It is nothing more than a weapon in disguise. It is ruining my life. When no one is looking, every crayon that I find, every one that is crushed on our hardwood floors, every one of them hidden or exposed, I throw them out; but no matter how often I do this, they keep turning up anyway. I think they must reproduce. The kids have colored everything in sight. I had to paint the walls to get rid of the crayon scribbles, and guess what? They're baaaack! And they don't only mar the walls and furniture. I spent hours doing my taxes, and contracts for my work, and even these did not escape the diabolical scribblings of my children. I was too exhausted to redo the taxes and contracts. They went out as is and people, including the IRS, will just have to put up with it."

He wasn't finished, just out-of-breath. "I never thought I'd see the day when the sight of a crayon made me ill. I HATE CRAYONS! EVERY LAST ONE OF THEM! They are my mortal enemy."

The shoppers who weren't afraid, pretended to shop nearby so they could eavesdrop on our conversation. They undoubtedly wondered why I hadn't dialed 9-1-1 yet.

While the poor man was frothing at the mouth and trying to catch his breath, I sympathized with him by getting my own complaints in. "I know just what you're going through. Only now that my children are grown am I getting to see the end of movies that I tried to watch when my kids were small. It was hopeless. It's as though kids want your attention every minute, and if you're trying to watch a movie, they sabotage it by standing in front of the screen, and if you get a call and try to catch up on family news, they give you no peace until you are forced to hang up. Nothing is the same when you have small children."

With clenched teeth and flushed cheeks, he said, "I know exactly what you are talking about. I am going through the same thing. I had the TV in one corner of my living room, and the kids would stand in a certain spot so that I could *never* see the picture. I figured there must be some reason, maybe the floor there is warm, or maybe the floor slants a little and it's the most comfortable spot for them. So one day I moved the TV to the other side of the room. Did that solve the problem? No! Now they stand in a new spot, right in front of the TV. It's like a conspiracy, or something. Why do they do this? I don't know if I'm going to survive. It's a nightmare!"

After a few more gasps and gulps, he continues, "Parenting is nothing more than slavery. They keep the wife and me hopping every minute. One will ask for a glass of milk, so I go in the kitchen, get a glass, take the milk out of the refrigerator, pour it in the glass, put the milk carton back in the refrigerator, and bring the milk to one kid. All of a sudden, *another* kid wants a glass of milk. It never ends, and you go back and forth, back and forth, going through the whole routine over and over. Why don't they all want the same thing at the same time? Are they afraid they'll make life a little easier for us?"

After seeing the condition of my landscaper friend in the supermarket, I checked the Obituary daily for the next year, but his name never showed up. I don't know what shape he is in, but he apparently managed to survive . . . unless, of course, he ended up in a mental ward somewhere. They don't list that in the newspapers.

My Friend, Mary

According to my friend, Mary, the motto for 1992 will be: "They just don't get it, do they?"

She is referring to the all-male Senate Committee that ruled in favor of Clarence Thomas over Anita Hill. Mary feels that a decision is not valid if it doesn't represent all of the people and it can't represent all of the people when there are no women in the Senate.

While she is expounding her theories on this national issue with great determination and conviction, she plops her 200 pounds down into my swivel chair—my personal chair, of all things—and reaches into my chocolate drawer behind her, helping herself repeatedly. (It was a dark day in my life when Mary discovered my secret drawer.)

In between bites, she is saying, "Chauvinism is still with us," chomp, chomp. "Men are running everything and important decisions that affect all of us are being made by men," chomp, chomp. "There is no balance of power and for a system to work there must be balance."

Speaking of balance, Mary has none. She has such a bulbous weight on her chest that she leans forward a little when she stands. She is a perfect candidate for breast reduction. Concerned, I once asked her, "Mary, at what age did you start to develop?" She answered, "I don't remember. All I know is, one morning when I was a teenager, I woke up, and my boobs were so big, I thought someone else was in the bed."

My top heavy friend reaches for more chocolate, then pushes herself back into the chair. The weight of her upper torso causes the chair to fall backward but her fall is broken by the open candy drawer. The top of the swivel chair is caught on that drawer—justice, if there ever was any. She looks like she's in a dentist's chair only she's a foot off the floor.

I rush over to her, but what can I do? She is twice my size. I pull and tug on the chair, but it is solidly locked onto my candy drawer. Maybe if one of the men she is railing out against were here, we wouldn't be in this predicament, but in light of her strong political opinions, I'm sure not going to mention that we could use the help of a man.

Strangely enough, her precarious situation does not quell the fervor of her political diatribe—nor her appetite for my candy, for that matter.

"Just look under your nose," chomp, chomp. I did, and all I could see under my nose was Mary on her back, hooked onto my secret candy drawer, the chocolate of which is rapidly vanishing.

"Just look under your nose in this town" she repeats. "Just because it's a woman running for office, they resorted to vandalism. Look what happened to the 225 signs she had put up. Why? Because they just can't stand to have a woman in power."

Mary tries to lift herself up, but quickly falls back down again. She is like a beetle on its back. I was disgusted, mostly about my dwindling chocolate supply. Perhaps if I could shut that drawer . . . .

I took hold of the back of her chair, and with adrenalin power, tried to lift it as I worked the drawer shut with my foot an inch at a time. I eventually succeeded, and Mary dropped to the floor with a loud thud. Jolting her pleased me to no end, her punishment for eating so much of my candy. Now lying flat on the floor, she is able to roll the chair sideways and crawl away.

She did not stop talking throughout this whole ordeal, nor did she stop chewing. "People are just not going to put up with endless inequities," chomp, chomp. "There's got to be change or we perish as a nation, as a state, and as a town."

Mary has crawled away from the chair on all fours and pulled herself back onto her feet by taking hold of the desk top. Without so much as a pause, she lifts the swivel chair, puts it back in the same place, and plops back down into it. Again, she is reaching far into my candy drawer, and continues her harangue.

"They just don't get it, do they?" and she is still chomping away.

"You haven't said much, Lucille. What do YOU think?"

"Mary, I don't know what the solution is to politics, religion, or life. All I know is, when you leave, I'm moving my candy to a new secret place where you can't find it."

Truth and Honesty

My friend in California is very proud of her two sons whom she describes as "fine young men who were brought up on Truth and Honesty."

She calls me up late one night and says, "I'm going in for surgery next week, so I thought I'd invite my sons and their wives over tonight for one last meal in case I don't make it." She then proceeds to tell me word for word the exact conversation that took place.

After a pleasant family dinner, she brings up the subject as tactfully as possible. "Remember, if anything happens to me, I want to be buried in my pink beaded dress, the one I wore at your wedding," and she nods towards her younger son.

And what does he say? "For goodness sake, Mom, give us a little credit. Think we'd bury you in jeans?"

A little jolted by his response, she pauses to catch her breath, then goes on, ". . .and I'd like a nice tombstone."

"Tombstone?" blurts the older son. "You're gonna get a marker like everyone else."

Again, she is startled, then regains her composure once more and continues. "I know you need a car," and she points to her younger son, "so I want you to have my car."

He answers, "That piece of junk? I'd sell it and put the money down on a *good* car."

Thoroughly disgusted, she turns away from her sons and addresses her daughter-in-law, "You are my size, so I want you to have my clothes."

"Not me," she answers, "I'm not wearing any dead woman's clothes."

My friend finally throws her hands in the air and bellows "Maybe you'd all better just send my body back home to New Jersey and let my family bury me!"

Both sons are horrified. "Be serious, Mom, do you know how expensive it is to ship a body across the country?"

Of course, I didn't help the situation any when I said, "You'll be lucky if they don't wrap you in burlap and bury you standing up. It's much cheaper that way."

After the operation, my friend calls me and says, "You know, after that last family dinner, I was determined to pull through if only out of spite, and I've never felt better. I'm gonna make my own arrangements and they can take it or leave it."

She doesn't say much about truth and honesty these days.

Out of the Mouths of Babes

My young friend, Jeanne, has a 5 year old son, and last Sunday, for the first time, she took little Joey to church with her while her husband, a musician who had worked late the night before, stayed home and rested. She would rather have gone alone to have a little rest away from child care, but it was the first time little Joey showed an interest in church, and she wanted to encourage it.

These are her exact words describing the experience:

"What an annoyance!" she complained. "Joey did nothing but fidget for the first twenty minutes, then he was supposed to go downstairs with all the other kids. Now I understand why they remove the kids from the service. It's to give mothers something to thank God for. But what do you think happened? He wouldn't go. Rather than create a scene, I let him stay with me, and he continued to squirm and fidget and look around and distract everyone around us.

"During one particularly quiet moment, there was a suspicious sound followed by an atrocious odor. I looked at Joey and he blurted out loudly, 'I didn't do it, it was him,' and he pointed to the young boy behind us, not realizing that his piercing voice carried, and everyone around could hear him. I repressed my laughter when the perpetrator behind us squirmed uneasily in his seat after being fingered by a small boy.

"Then what does Joey do? A baritone choir member sang a solo, and really, Lucille, I could understand why the back of the program read: Wanted, choir members, especially men. He had a vibrato a yard wide that made you seasick. The minute he opened his mouth, his voice cracked. Joey, who is pretty musical like his father, looked at this singer, looked at me, and began to giggle. Once again, I had to use all my willpower to hold back laughter. All of this repression was giving me a stomach ache.

"At one point, everything was quiet except for the minister offering a prayer. Everyone's head was bowed, when suddenly you could hear a resounding rat-tat-tat-tat-tat. Joey figured out a way to keep the seat next to him bouncing.

"Then he poked me with one finger and said, 'Mommy, he was at our house,' referring to the minister, and from then on, he poked me every time he saw a friend or a neighbor that we knew. He'd say, 'Look, Mommy, there's Mrs. So-and-so. Look, Mommy, there's Mr. So-and-so.'

"I can't tell you how aggravating church was that day. Joey didn't let up for one minute. Even as we were leaving, Joey looked back at the building and said, 'Mommy, church is a jerk-off.'

"No sooner was I relieved in the knowledge that Joey was so bored having to sit there for an hour, he would not want to go again, when Joey piped up as we were approaching our house, 'Can I come with you next week, Mommy?'"

After listening intently to Jeanne's painful account of Joey's first time at church, I am very grateful that my kids are grown.

The Conversion

Lisa had been inviting me to visit her church group for a long time, a small group that held services at a VFW hall. I kept promising her I would go, so one Sunday I decided to surprise her and just show up. It wasn't easy looking for a place that is stuck way back on a side street off another side street, but I finally found it. I was impressed by the number of cars in the parking lot. Lisa's church really must have grown, I thought.

I entered the building. A man seated at a table in the foyer in front of the main hall doorway glanced up at me and said, "Chree dollaz."

How interesting, I thought. Things must be changing in the new churches. Instead of an Offering during the service, you give at the door. Maybe that's more efficient.

I gave him the money and stepped around him into the large room. A very pleasant lady greeted me with, "Glad you could come," which I thought was a very nice friendly welcome, only . . . something puzzled me. Why was she wearing a funny little paper hat with an elastic band around her chin. Am I in the right VFW Hall?

My first impulse was to leave, but I was pushed ahead by the enthusiastic crowd behind me. Once in the large hall, someone-I don't know who-put a paper plate in my hand and herded me into a line.

Two men that I was sure were the Pastor and Elder, were wearing a large white full body apron and a tall white baker's hat. They were working feverishly behind a long table. If nothing else, this was certainly a down-to-earth church where the leaders serve the congregation. Not a bad practice! One of them put freshly made pancakes on my plate and the other, picture perfect sausages. Bewildered, I brought my food over to a table and looked around for Lisa.

A friendly couple who acted like they've known me all of my life joined me. At the appropriate moment, I asked, cautiously, "Uh . . . when do services begin?"

Their forks stopped in midair and they looked at me strangely, then looked at each other.

I continued, "I . . . uh . . . came here to attend church."

The man, Mr. Personality himself, with a mouth packed with pancake, blurted out, "Ya want a blessing? I'll give ya a blessing," and he laughed himself silly until he choked on his food.

And then it happened . . .

Someone floating around came over to our table and put a little paper hat on my head. Another person following behind them pinned brightly colored buttons on my chest. A third person gave me a ruler and pencils. Whatever for, I don't know, but all I know is that whatever religion it was, I was now officially a member.

After a second helping of pancakes, with no sign of a service about to begin, it was time to go. The hostess gave me a handful of literature on my way out and wiggled her fingers at me while chirping cheerily, "See you tonight."

I drove straight to Lisa's house, still wearing my paper hat and colorful buttons. I left the ruler and pencils in the car. She took one look at me and said, "What happened to you?"

"Don't ask me," I answered. "All I know is, I went over to your VFW hall to visit your church group, and when I went in I was a Christian, and when I came out, I was a Politician."

"Oh, no!" she shrieked. "We rent that hall with the stipulation that at election time, we forego our morning service so they can have their political pancake breakfast. But try to come tonight. We're having our services there at 7."

"Can't. Now that I'm in politics, I have to help out with the election."

FAMILY

My Son, Myself

My son never seemed to refer to people by name. He would refer to everyone by their most distinguishing feature. He didn't do it in a deprecating way, or to hurt anyone. There was no malice involved. It was simply his way of identifying them. Even when he was a boy, he'd say, of his baby sister, "Mom, Diaper Rash is awake." If anything, there was a little humor involved.

I used to teach piano and I had one student who had a big round face. When my son saw her coming up the driveway, he'd say, "Mom, Pumpkin Head is here."

We once rented out a room downstairs, but had to ask the person to move because of the clutter, the dirt, and the smell of half-eaten rotting food that permeated the whole house. I agreed to allow him to leave a bag of clothes to be picked up a few days later. When he came to pick up the clothes, my son answered the door then shouted, "Mom! Dirt Bag is here."

There was a hefty complaining neighbor who was always shrieking about one thing or another. My son used to say, "Fat's at it again."

His descriptions were always right on, so you always knew who he was talking about. However, while many of the things he said were humorous, I couldn't help but wonder where on earth he learned to talk that way.

Then last week I found a copy of an old letter
of mine to my closest friend Jeanne, written right
after I moved out of a Queens neighborhood. That's
where we bought our first house on a tree-lined
street so that the children could enjoy a quiet, clean,
decent neighborhood. I moved into this area with
great excitement and high expectancy. This illusion
did not last long. In time, I learned to view these 50
foot plots as grave sites with above-ground caskets.
We then moved as far away as we could from there
without losing access to New York City.

The first thing I told Jeanne in the letter was that
Total from the old neighborhood called me. Total was
my name for the woman next door to me there who
had so many illnesses, she was like a walking Merck
manual. She was bedridden when her husband was
around, but I noticed that when he was gone, she was
up and around and vigorously folding laundry.

Every time I saw her, she'd complain about a different illness, so one day we got to talking about—
what else?—her health and I asked her how many
illnesses she had. For the next hour, she gave me a
rundown beginning with her head where she said
there was a plate in her skull that was put there when
a thick glass door smashed her head in. She pointed
to her forehead and said she gets migraines. Moving
down, she said she had double vision which, incidentally, didn't seem to hinder her from dialing my
number. Then there were the nasal and throat problems; a hearing problem; a ton of allergies; and an
arthritic neck. Then there was the TMJ—some sort
of jaw disorder; dental problems, plus. I can't pos-

sibly list every single disorder as she traveled down her torso, but no bone or organ or tract escaped her list.

She was wearing sandals, so by the time she got down to her feet, I could see that nine of her toes did not escape calamity. All but one big toe had been injured in one way or another and were painted with mercurochrome. I stared at this healthy, plump big toe that had escaped the ravages of her accident proneness and hypochondria. That one big toe stood as a monument to Hope for potential health in this woman.

Just then her husband came home. He was so distracted by my unexpected presence since they very seldom had visitors, that as he was walking awkwardly past his wife saying, "Hello, Lucille," he accidentally stepped on that one healthy toe. With that, she was totaled. That healthy toe, the very point from which she could begin her trek back to health, was gone. All hope for good health was gone, thus giving rise to my nickname for her, Total, because in my eyes, she was totaled.

To get on with the letter, I told Jeanne that Total was talking to Olive Oyl, who lived on the other side of her, two houses over from me when I lived there.

Olive Oyl was a tall woman with legs like broomsticks that I had never before seen on anything before except a pigeon. Whenever I saw her, I would automatically visualize a message tied to one of them. She is the only person I ever met who was petrified of being alone. Her husband had to justify every moment away from her because "He knows I can't stand to be alone!" The strain of this pressure showed on his face. The one night that her husband had to attend the company party, she asked me to stay with her. It's the first and only time I ever had to adult-sit. That poor man looked forward to going to work everyday to get away from her.

So, in my letter, I tell Jeanne that Olive Oyl was telling Total the activities of Mother Goose across the street. Mother Goose was a woman who had so many children she didn't know what to do. To get away from her kids, she'd go up and down the street gossiping with any available ear, bringing tales from door to door. Not even the mailman could escape her perpetually moving mouth. One day, her 40 year old prematurely old husband came home, sat in a chair and died. Everyone knew why.

By the time I finished reading my letter to Jeanne, there was no more mystery about my son's expressions. He had simply turned into me.

Ya Gotta Hand It To 'Em

I had a reunion with an old friend, and she showed me a letter that I had written her when my son was pre-teen. He went from disagreeable to perverse, which was an improvement. We re-read the letter together and laughed ourselves silly over it. The letter went like this:

Dear Jeanne,

Motherhood is more enjoyable now that my son is less of a demanding child and more of a jokester. Like today my son walked up to me and put a very cold hand up to my forehead and said, 'I think you have a fever, Mom.' No sooner was I about to compliment him on his concern and compassion when the hand dropped out of his sleeve to the floor. I almost had a heart attack. It was a rubber hand with a bloody wrist that he bought Saturday at the fair. It gave me an idea.

My friend, Gina, has a brilliant son, a promising nuclear physicist who was home from college on a school break that week. This kid tries to be funny, but his humor is like his driving—slow and plodding. When you call there, he tries to startle you by answering something like, "Remote synthesizer control room," but I am wise to him. Instead of acting like I have the wrong number, which he counts on, I simply say, "Let me speak to your mother."

Anyway, I had to drop something off at his house and could hardly wait to go. I brought my son with me and told him to bring his bloody hand. So we walked in and the whole family is sitting there at the dinner table, a perfect time to get everybody's attention. My son walks up to the genius and says, "Shake." The young physicist puts his hand out without looking and ends up holding a detached hand. The parents stopped eating and stared at their son who was standing there awkwardly holding a bloody rubber hand. This genius knows what to do with a blackboard full of complicated formulas, but he didn't know what to do with a bloody rubber hand. His siblings began to giggle. I couldn't help adding, "That's what you get for answering the phone the way you do." Everyone ended up choking with laughter. It was so successful that I decided to keep this good thing going.

On our way home, we stopped by Rudy and Stella's house. We waited in joyful expectation for their son, Jim to get off the phone. When he did, my son said, "Shake, Jim." If you could see the look on Jim's face when he found himself holding a rubber hand! He didn't smile; he didn't frown. He just stood there looking like someone took a bat to his head. His sister screamed at the sight of a bloody hand and ran from the room. Her reaction was even funnier than her brother's petrified stare.

They led us out the door pretty quickly, but we were back in no time. You see, as we were walking to our car, my son stuck the rubber hand back in his sleeve then decided to salute with it. When he brought his hand up to his head, the hand flew up in the air and landed on their roof. We weren't going to leave without this wonderful weapon, so we were back at their door. When their daughter opened the door, she took one look at my son and screamed and ran away for the second time—and he wasn't even holding the bloody hand. It made my son and me feel powerful that we brought such delightful terror to this tranquil household.

Rudy and Stella groaned at the sight of us, but then helped us figure out way to get the hand off the roof. Once retrieved, my son put on a show for their neighbors by attaching the bloody hand to his neck and screaming like he was being strangled. What a convincing performance he put on!

Finally, he put the hand back in his sleeve so that it hung down like he had a broken wrist. To everyone's relief, we finally left. My son and I were never before so happy together. We were like a mother/son Bonnie and Clyde.

We then went by Larry and Florence's house. Larry took it very well, especially the part where my son went a step further and put it on the inside of the sink with the fingers over the edge then began screaming that a monster was climbing out of the drain. He had them in stitches.

The horror theme changed when my son stuck the fake index finger up his nose so that it looked like this bloody severed hand was picking his nose. That did it! It was time to call it a day. We went home where he tortured his baby sister with the rubber hand for the next half hour—the end of a perfect day.

So, how are things there in your *normal* household, Jeanne? Give me a call.

Your friend,
Lucille

Early Teenage Years

By my son's 14th birthday, I took a good long look at him and came to the conclusion that Early Teenager is the link that *should* have been missing.

It wasn't always this way. He was a wonderful child and a good student . . . right up to his first pimple. It was a startling transformation. He didn't walk anymore, he swaggered, and nothing looks more peculiar than a swagger with legs that look like a giant wishbone. His speech was also impaired. His sentences became shorter and shorter until he spoke in grunts and belches. Incredibly enough, his friends understood him. They ALL spoke that way.

One day after school, my son and his friends asked me to drive them to the store. I couldn't believe the items they bought: special dandruff shampoo, hair crème, toothpaste, mouthwash, deodorant, and last, but not least, foot powder. It cost a small fortune. Despite all of this personal hygiene and grooming, they still smelled the same. No product is powerful enough to neutralize the bodily chemicals oozing from teenage pores. When my son and his class-mates piled into my car, the air was instantly filled with "essence of sweaty sneaker." Sometimes, it got so bad that I could swear I was locked in an animal cage.

Their conversations consisted of how they out-smarted their teachers that day. There was one poor teacher upon whom they heaped most of their abuse, a nervous older man with a loud, resonant, baritone voice. They'd get this man into such an incoherent state that he hardly knew what he was saying. He'd raise three fingers in the air and thunder, "You've got THREE choices! Either you go to your seat or you go to the office!"

One of their special techniques with this particular teacher went like this:

Teacher: GO...TO...THE...OFFICE! (You have to picture him through their eyes. They said his face and his clothing were completely wrinkled, and the crotch of his pants sagged almost to his knees. His right hand was a claw-like baton which he thrust forward with every word.)

Teenager: I didn't do nuthin'. (which was the standard teenage answer.)

Teacher: I...SAID...GO...TO...THE...OFFICE!

Teenager: But I just WENT to the Library. (Notice the switch to confuse the teacher.)

Teacher: I...SAID...GO...TO...THE...LIBRARY! THAT'S IT! YOU'RE GOING TO THE LIBRARY.... NOW GO!...GO!GO! GO! OUT!...OUT!

The only thing worse than the unbearable noise level when the boys were in my car was the silence. Their silence was deadly. It meant that one of them 'cut one' and they were waiting for it to reach the driver – me. The minute I gagged, choked, and open up the windows, they would laugh with voice-cracking hysteria. I often thought of installing an Eject Button on my dashboard connected to the sun window so that when they did this, I could just press the button, and they'd go flying out the roof.

When these boys slept over, I learned never to open the door to my son's room, not even a crack. You see, they had strange contests, and the few times I stuck my head in, it was like sticking my head in a septic tank.

There was a time when I had complete faith in my son's physical coordination. At age three, people gathered to watch him swim. He rode a two wheeler early. At six he could handle a three-speeder. At ten, I bought him a ten-speeder. He mastered it so quickly that at age 11, I got him a motorcycle, an SL 70. Again, he mastered it. But then . . . that pimple showed up, and everything changed. At least once a day, he'd trip on the stairs. Once, both of his big toes were swollen at the same time from unrelated causes. I booked him every three weeks at the emergency room because with regularity, he needed medical attention for a sprain or a possible fracture.

It wasn't even safe to be in the same room with him. Rarely did he walk by me without bumping into me or stepping on my feet, not foot, feet. His foot was so big, it covered both of mine. If I was washing dishes and he reached for something in the cabinet above, he'd invariably bump my head, elbow me in the breast, drop the object either on me or in the dishwater which then splashed in my face, any or all of the above.

I received a note from school: Your son has been late 27 times. I wasn't sure they meant that year or that term. Actually, it was surprising that he showed up at all, after all, he had better things to do, like practicing wheelies. (That's when you pull your motorcycle up so that you are riding along on the rear wheel.) He told his friends that I could do this with my Volvo Station Wagon. They would goad me all the way home from school in my car with their bullfrog voices chanting, "C'mon, Ms. R, let's see ya do a wheelie."

Once, a neighbor called and asked me why I sounded so weak. For one thing, I hadn't recovered from the ordeal of rushing my son to the emergency room, and his three weeks weren't even up yet! And what's worse, I made him stay in all day to convalesce. He stepped on me so many times that I have only three moving toes left. He lifted a bag of three one-quart cans of oil and turned suddenly, bumping into me and bruising my arm. He accidentally spilled hot oil on my hand and I have a painful blister developing. I was so totally wiped out from the energy it took to stay alive, that when another neighbor called to tell me that her son ran away from home, all I could think was, "Some people have all the luck."

A friend consoled me with, "Hang in there. Their accident proneness leaves by the time they're sixteen." All I could see was, two more years of this? And *then* what terrible thing replaces it?

They say we spend the first part of our lives escaping our parents, and the second part escaping our children. Let's hope that the third part makes up for the first two parts.

My Daughter's Wedding

The first week in July I went to my daughter's wedding in Puerto Vallarta, Mexico, my first trip in years. First of all, by the beginning of May, my cataracts were taken care of and that left plenty of time before the wedding to heal. There was a snag, though. After three failed attempts to get the correct prescription for astigmatism, the wedding was upon me and I was forced to go despite my blurred vision. My sister went with me, and she's deaf. Between my inability to see and her inability to hear, it was a miracle that we made it to Mexico at all. Had the pilot announced that we just landed in London, it would not have surprised me one bit.

Friends of my daughter came from all over the United States to attend her wedding. Most were musicians and some were from her scuba diving group in California. I don't know what they imagined I was like, but they were all shocked at my appearance. I guess when you see a rock singer with fifty orange and yellow tiny braids down to her waist, and an unconventional outfit suited to the Rock stage, you somehow don't expect her mother to look like an executive secretary. Heads went back and forth between my daughter and me like they were at a tennis match.

The beautiful villa was set right in the mountainside overlooking the bay. It might have been a perfect setting if I had not been compelled to keep a watchful eye out for the lizard-like geckos slithering across the ceiling above my head. I didn't mind the iguana that showed up daily above the balcony and stood absolutely still on a branch, trying to look like part of the tree. He became my sort-of mascot and we had an understanding. I told him straight, "Yo, I know you're there. Limbs don't have eyes and a long tail."

The one thing everyone had in common by the second day was a backache. All the rooms were delightfully air conditioned, but the mattresses were like slabs of concrete. By the fifth day, everyone was groaning in pain, but tried to keep a cheerful countenance for my daughter's sake. She worked so hard to make her wedding a success.

The kitchen staff didn't understand a word of English, so we did a lot of pointing and nodding, but their guacamole was the best I have ever had in my life. In fact, I don't think I ever had real guacamole until then. And believe it or not, they also made the best bacon I ever tasted, crisp with no fat. I couldn't figure that one out.

Part of the villa deal was to provide a hairdresser for the bride. They were kind enough to include me in this package. However, their Mexican hairdresser did not know how to do American hair. Not to embarrass him, my daughter waited till he left and re-did her hair herself. She looked beautiful! I, on the other hand, looked like my head was caught in a blender. And there wasn't enough time to wash the thick layer of hair spray that made it impossible to re-coif.

While my hair was being massacred, the wedding band arrived dressed in their native Mexican regalia. Not one of them was under 75. They unpacked their instruments—three violins, two guitars, a bass guitar (with the fat body held horizontally) and a couple of trumpets—and they lined up against the veranda wall downstairs where they awaited the appearance of the bride and her mother at the top of the ornate marble staircase.

As my daughter and I began our descent, I became very sentimental, after all, this was my one and only daughter. I was on the verge of crying at the top of the stairs when the band started to play. The music was so loud and out-of-tune, my mind shifted back to my daughter's fifth grade band concert where the kids all started together when the band director gave the signal, but after that, they were on their own.

Instead of tears, I could not stop laughing all the way down the stairs. My daughter kept reprimanding me by squeezing my hand, a silent message that said, "Pull yourself together, Mama!" but it only made me laugh harder. The band played with such gusto, like a fanfare before a bull fight, but you didn't want to hurt their feelings by saying anything. As one of the musician guests later said, "I have a new definition of a minor second. It's two Mexican violinists playing in unison."

After the beautiful and moving wedding ceremony, the reception band came. They were very good. The keyboard player used nice changes and a lot of tasty improvisation. The bass player sang "The Shadow of Your Smile" with a thick Spanish accent. It made us smile, but it wasn't nearly as amusing as the Asian woman who sang, "Fry Me To The Moon."

The next few days were spent sight-seeing and bargaining for souvenirs. It went something like this:

an article began at $20.00 and the dealer would say, "Because I like you, I give to you for $15.00." Then you'd say, "Because you have such a nice face, I will give you $10.00." But what really clinches a deal is when you start walking away, then you get it for $8.00; a new experience for me. I never bought this way.

One evening we all went to the most famous club in the area, predictably called, "The Iguana." During our meal, there was this strange sound overhead. We thought the ceiling was collapsing. It was the noise of the rain on the tin roof. It was not only loud, competing with the stage show, but the roof was so flimsy, with rows of bubbly tin, that everyone in the restaurant was sprayed.

As for the floor show, you really got your money's worth. Their loud songs and foot stomping dances went on endlessly. If you happened to sit at a table near the stage, as I did, you'd have to protect your food from the beads and fluff that went flying through the air into your food during such lively dancing. So you had to protect your head from the rain and your food from the debris. It kept us all occupied.

The dancers were attractive and agile, though the men were skinny as a rail and the women, buxom. When they kicked up their legs and twirled their skirts, you saw calves that were like giant cabbages. They were all troopers, though. They ignored the rain on their heads, and danced right through the beads underfoot without slipping.

I can't end without mentioning the Mexican taxi drivers. Their driving would scare a New York cab driver. To make matters worse, most of the roads are cobblestone, so by the time you reached your destination, all your teeth are broken. It happened to rain that night we went out, so the cobblestones were wet and slippery. Since the villa is up in the mountain, and all cobblestone roads leading there were wet, the dilapidated taxis could not make the hill. The more the driver gave it the gas, the more the wheels spun and the taxi slid backwards. One musician jumped out and walked to the Villa. The next day he said, "Well, I didn't feel like dying at the hands of a Mexican taxi driver."

One cab driver was either very funny, or knew only one word in English. His driving was so erratic, a musician asked, "When did you learn to drive?"

The cabbie said, "Today."

And the musician asked, "When did you get your license?"

The driver said, "Today."

When the five days were up, I was ready to go home. It's nice to get away, but it's even nicer to come home. I packed my souvenir sandals, necklace, and towels that that I bought that said Puerto Vallarta, and was ready to leave. Fortunately, a musician and his wife had the same flight as my sister and I, so we didn't have to worry about reading signs and hearing announcements. They led us through terminals like seeing-eye dogs.

I was so relieved to get home to my own bed where my back could heal, and so happy that my one and only daughter had such a memorable wedding, real memorable.

The Mama Quartet

I

Mama immigrated to the United States with her husband at a very young age. She wanted so much to learn English, so she somehow acquired a huge unabridged dictionary and copied words every time she had a free moment. She *did* manage to learn to write well enough, phonetically, to leave notes. One was for the mailman: "Pleez put mail in door slok." Apparently he knew what a door slok was because the mail did show up inside her front door.

One woman was always asking to use her phone, so one day she got a note, too: "If you want to use a fone, go to the corner."

Whenever she wrote me, she'd sign it, "Your Mother," then under that, she'd sign her full name. I tried to tell her from time to time that I know who my mother is, that she doesn't have to sign her full name, but I don't think she ever believed me. She just kept signing her full name.

She never failed to send me a birthday card. Trouble is, they were usually cards that someone else sent her. It wasn't unusual for me to get a birthday card that said Happy Mother's Day, and signed by someone else in the family, but coming from my mother's address. The last card she ever sent me had a picture of a monk in a brown robe with a flame coming out of the top of his head. The caption said, Saint Jude, patron saint of the hopeless cases. I have tried to convince myself that she just didn't realize, but there's always that doubt way back in my mind.

One day while I was visiting, she turned the television on and I sat on the couch with her to watch it. I was curious to see how much she understood.

In the movie, a man killed his wife, then the background music swelled to a booming crescendo, expressing the maniacal emotions of this murderer.

My mother turned to me and said, "Look at that! First he kills his wife, then he plays the radio."

II

The Meanest Thing Mama Ever Did

In keeping with the people of her generation, my old widowed Mama had an altar on her dresser. There were at least fifty saints of all sizes, shapes, and material: tall, short, fat, skinny, glass, plaster. Strangely enough, though, they all had blue eyes, and no matter where you went in her bedroom, those eyes followed you.

One day, after the long drive to visit her, I was resting on her bed, staring at her crowded dresser. I became aware of three lit bulbs the size of cherry tomatoes in front of the altar, something like seven watts each.

I called my mother into the room and asked, "Mama, what is the meaning of those three bulbs?

She answered, "The first one is for Jesus, Mary and Joseph, and all the Saints.

I looked at the bulb, then at her, then back at the bulb and said, "All that on seven watts?"

She continued, "The second one is for all the dead in purgatory."

If I thought there were a lot of people on bulb one, can you imagine how many people lived and died from the beginning of time that are crowded on that second bulb? It was staggering!

Then I thought about the third bulb. I couldn't imagine what was left.

"Mama, what is that third bulb for?"

"That one is for Papa."

"PAPA? Papa got his own bulb???" She gave him more wattage than all the Saints, even.

Six months later, when I visited again, I noticed that there were only two bulbs on her altar. I knew she wouldn't cancel bulb one or two, so I asked, "Mama, what did you do with Papa?"

She said, "Well, one day I was sitting in the kitchen thinking about something he did to me years ago, and I got so mad, I went in there, and I unscrewed his bulb!"

III

The Physical Exam

During another visit to my mother, while we were at the table having breakfast, I said, "Mama, you're getting on in age, now. Don't you think you ought to have a physical?" She had never been to a doctor in her life, not even for the birth of her nine babies.

She answered, "Oh, your sister brought me a few months ago."

"You never told me. What did the doctor say?"

"He said, 'Don't eat any eggs and don't eat any bread.'"

Meanwhile, we're sitting there having eggs and toast, so I tried to put guilt trip on her and said, "Mama, what would the doctor say if he saw you sitting there eating eggs and bread?"

She shrugged her shoulder and answered, "I don't know. He died."

IV

The Healing

When she was having trouble with her vision, she told me that she had the cataract operation on one eye.

I said, "Mama, why did they only do one eye?"

She answered, "The doctor said the other eye was too old."

"Too old? Aren't your eyes the same age, Mama?"

Then, since she was a religious woman, I said, "Listen, why don't we pray about it? God can heal your eyes. Look what He did for Sarah, Abraham's wife. He gave her a baby at your age."

My mother thought about that for awhile, then said, "Gee, I hope He doesn't do that to me."

PETS

King Kong Revisited

When an attractive single woman of 28 speaks in endearing terms about Max, calls him the best thing that's ever happened to her in her whole life, and kisses his picture over and over, what do we assume?

Wrong.

Max is her new horse.

Late one night Patty said, "I'm worried about Max. He has a cut on his ankle that should be tended to daily and I haven't been able to get to the stables since last Saturday. Take a ride with me."

Next thing I knew, we're heading north in her open truck, with the sweltering air blowing grime in our faces. Within an hour, the scenery changed from restaurants and street lights to pitch black dirt roads, and the temperature dropped 10 degrees.

The farm, with houses and barns barely visible against the dark sky, was quiet. It was well past everyone's bedtime, both owners and animals.

After a half mile of pot holes, Patty pulled up to one of the smaller barns, jumped out of the truck and, like an old farm hand, knew just where the light switch was in the pitch black barn. Four hairy heads peered sleepily from their stalls. They were definitely not happy to see us.

Patty opened Max's stall door, slid a halter over his head and led him to the cross ties in the center of the barn where horses are anchored for grooming, all the while showering him with a profusion of kisses, and in between kisses, exclaiming "Isn't he beautiful?" She didn't care that I didn't answer and never noticed that I was protecting myself behind a barn post. If this gigantic beast broke free, it could crush the two of us like ants.

This horse was so big, Patty was only up to the shoulder. As she began working on him, it was like watching Fay Wray groom King Kong and Patty wasn't at all intimidated by this 2,000 pound mass of chestnut brown rippling muscle. When she dug into Max's coat, first with a rubber brush to dislodge the dirt and loose hair, and then with a regular brush to sweep the tufts onto the ground, Max acted as annoyed as King Kong did when he was atop the Empire State building and the fighter planes were buzzing around him. Max would turn his head all the way around and look at Patty with furrowed brow as if to say, "What on earth are you doing? Leave me alone!" And then, every so often, she'd stick her fingers in his mouth and playfully jiggle his rubbery lips. Max would get a pained look on his face as if to say, "When is this going to end?"

Fearlessly, Patty got right under Max and bent his legs back to clean each hoof, commenting, "My farrier replaces these shoes every six to eight weeks," totally ignoring the fact that Max winced with every twist and jab. She even polished his hooves and, like a doting mother, said "There, now you have nice new shoes." But Max didn't seem thrilled about it. He just wanted to get back to bed.

I thought for sure that Max was going to bolt when she stung his cut with medicine. He drew his leg up under his body and his head swiveled around, giving her a look that said, "What ARE you doing to me?" To add insult to injury, Patty decided Max needed exercise, so she pulled this sleepy hulk out into the dark and trotted back and forth, running alongside him with ongoing horse patter, "That's good, Max, just one more time."

By the time she put him back in his stall, he was so tired and possibly angry, he put his nose to the back wall and his rear end toward Patty. And the other three horses followed suit and turned their backsides to her, also; after all, she kept *them* up, too. All the way back, I kept thinking of the last line in King Kong, "It was Beauty that killed the Beast."

When we got back to my house, I unlocked the door and started to enter. Patty was entering right behind me when she let out such a bloodcurdling scream that neighbors' lights began coming on. Not knowing what this terror was, I fled and hid behind a bush with her. My imagination went wild, and my heart pounded with fear. What was it? A burglar? A serial killer? But I really couldn't see anything.

"What is it? What is it" I cried, as I looked all about for the intruder. There!" she screamed, and pointed upward.

"Where?" I couldn't see anything.

"There."

Suspended from the top of the open doorway was a near-invisible strand of web, on the end of which dangled a spider the size of a period. It occurred to me that this woman who fearlessly poked and mauled and got underneath a two thousand pound horse was terrified of a tiny, tiny spider that you would need a magnifying glass to see.

So I rewrote the last line of King Kong. "While it was Beauty (Patty) that killed the Beast (Max), in the final analysis, t'was the Beast (the tiny spider) that killed the Beauty (Patty)."

Don't Give Your Dog a Bad Name

There is definitely a correlation between a dog's name and its disposition. I have learned this startling fact the hard way: on-the-job traumas. When I get a call to tune a piano, I first ask if they have a dog, and if so, what its name is. The name often determines whether I take the job or not.

I have never had trouble with dogs that have names like Tiffany, Beauty, and Cuddles. These tiny trembling tyrants with satin bows in their neatly coifed crowns are the pampered rulers of the household. Who can be terrorized by their outburst of yips performed perfunctorily to earn their keep? One step in their direction and they scoot away like disoriented centipedes.

In this category of petite pooches are names like Bubbles, Peaches, double syllable ones like FiFi, JoJo, and FruFru and, of course, French names, like Pierre and Roulette. I would not hesitate to take these tuning jobs. HOW...EV...ER . . . if the dog's name is Champ, that's out. I know all about Champ.

Champ

I rang Champ's doorbell early one morning, and in a flash, he lunged at the window, barking furiously, with his paws on the window pane and his eyes up near the curtain rod. How big was this dog, anyway, I wondered, as I stood on the porch and looked up at it.

I had second thoughts about ringing again when the door opened a crack. A woman's voice whispered "Move slowly or he attacks." I should have run for my life then, but I didn't. It took me half an hour to inch my way from the front door to the piano. Champ, this big menacing brute, a Boxer who could probably eat a hundred pound human in two bites, never took his red beady eyes off me for one moment. Then his mistress let him sniff me all over—such indignity—and when she felt that I was no longer a stranger to him, she left the room.

It was hard to turn my back on Champ, but what could I do? I can't tune a piano with my back to it, so I turned around. I could still feel his staring eyes watching every move I made. I leaned into the piano to check the action when this monstrous mongrel, this bulldog on stilts, this carnivore, came up behind me like a bulldozer and lifted me a foot off the floor then dropped me.

The woman ran in when she heard me crash back to the floor. She sized up the situation and looked fondly at her smug beast, then at me, and said, "He likes you."

He likes me? Annoyed, I almost said, "I'll bet you wouldn't say that if your husband did that to me."

Bear

On another job, the real estate woman said, "I have to go show a house. I'll be right back. Don't worry about Bear. He's locked in a room upstairs."

The name gave me an uneasy feeling, but I convinced myself that I was safe, after all, he's locked in a room. Then at one point I had to go out to my car to get a special tool. When I re-entered the house, Bear went wild. My re-entry obviously constituted a break-in to him.

After the most frantic footwork overhead, there was a loud crash and a furious flow of atonal vocal sounds that would be the envy of any dodecaphonic composer of the twentieth century. In a flash, an enormous chestnut brown mass shot down the stairs with legs stretched straight out in front of him and his rear end slapping every third step. If there ever was a crazed animal, this was it.

Bear hit the wall at the foot of the stairs and ricocheted toward me after running into two support posts and a table. I recall quite vividly the thought that entered my mind: I always knew that someday I would die, but I had no idea it would be as dog food.

After pulling myself into my synthetic fur coat like a frightened turtle, I cried, in a pathetically wavering voice, "Upstairs, Bear."

Bear slid to a halt within inches of me and looked up at my face curiously, as if to say, "How does she know my name? Do I know her?"

Again, a little stronger, and maybe slightly bolder, I repeated, "Upstairs, Bear." I was astonished that the beast knew his name, and for a dog the size of a pony, it obeyed.

He turned and started walking toward the stairs, looking back at me several times with a quizzical look on his face as if still wondering, "Do I know her?"

Even with Bear gone, I was still visibly shaken and holding onto a support post when the lady came home. All I could say was, "Bear paid me a visit."

"That's impossible!" she cried, and she stomped up the stairs. She was startled by what she found. The locked door was broken clean off its hinges and Bear was curled up and snoring peacefully in another room. Her final words were that old familiar line of the illuminated unbeliever in a Class B monster movie, "Can you beat that!"

My Conclusion

Dogs with human names like Penny, Alfred, and Gretchen, are all bark, but if you raise your arm, they run like hell. With dogs named Champ, Bear, Duke, Brutus, King, Thor, and the like, I do not raise my arm, I raise my price.

Bootsie

I had just finished tuning my friend Louise's piano and while we were having a cup of tea, I started complaining about the rash of dog abuses I had been experiencing on the job of late.

On one job, I ring the bell and this lady opens the door a crack and says, "Walk slowly, he attacks." Meanwhile, this huge dog is barking furiously in the background and his voice has a deep loud bass range. It was frightening! It took me half an hour to get from the front door to the piano, all the while that camel is sitting there with his eyes focused on my every move. Then when I took the front panel off the piano and was leaning into it to inspect, Champ comes up behind me and lifts me a foot in the air. When the lady hears me drop to the floor, she comes into the room and what does she do? She looks at the dog fondly and says, "Champ likes you." If that dog had been a human, it would be in jail for sexual harassment for what it did to me, and all she could say was, "He likes you." Who cares? Was I supposed to be flattered that her dog liked me?

Then there's this other woman who leaves me at the piano and says, "I'll be right back. Don't worry about Bear, he's locked in a room upstairs." *That* dog breaks a door down, comes flying down the stairs, and wants to have me for dinner. This is another dog that would have been arrested for assault if it had been a person.

And then there are those smaller dogs who stick their snout in my bag and run off with my tools and you have to chase them all over the house.

Louise listens patiently to my stream of complaints and then says, kindly, "Lucille, you just don't understand dogs. You don't know how wonderful they are. I want you to meet Bootsie." So she takes me to another part of the house where this short-hair medium-size black and tan dog with a very pointy snout starts barking her head off. If there were such a thing as a doggy Barber Shop Quartet, this one would be the soprano.

The three of us walk back to the kitchen and Louise says, "Let me show you how protective Bootsie is. You'll soon change your mind about dogs. With great confidence, she says, "Attack me."

"Attack you? How do I do that? I never attacked anyone, before."

"Grab my arm," she orders, so I grab her arm and we begin tugging back and forth, keeping a watchful eye on Bootsie.

First Bootsie begins barking furiously, then she begins running in a circle, like she's crazed. A lot of good *that's* going to do if a burglar attacks, I thought.

Louise says, "Pull harder, Lucille!" so here we are tugging even harder back and forth. Bootsie goes from chasing her tail into a bounce, like she's on a pogo stick, springing higher and higher in the air, and with each bounce, she is squealing like a stuck pig.

I'm waiting to see what this *protective* cur is going to do to change my opinion, so when she bounces as high as our shoulders, she opens her jaw and in a state of uncontrollable frenzy, she lets out a scream-bark, and bites aimlessly in the air. The trouble is, she bites Louise.

Everything stops. Louise is in shock. She is staring at the teeth marks on her arm in stunned silence, then slowly turns her glare to Bootsie, who is standing there in fearful anticipation, ready to flee. Everything is quiet and still, like the eye of the tornado. Tension fills the air and I sense something is about to erupt.

Louise's whole countenance changes and she takes off after Bootsie, who is yelping and running for her life. This house is designed so that you can run in a circle from the kitchen to the dining room through the living room and back to the kitchen. Louise is like a wild animal chasing after Bootsie, who is squealing at the top of her soprano voice, as Louise is screaming 'NO, Bootsie! That's NOT what you're supposed to do! That's NOT what you're supposed to do!"

While this high speed circular chase is going on, I grab my tool bag and run for the front door. Even as I jumped in my car, I could still hear this frantic duet going on in the house, with Louise still shouting, "NO! That's NOT what you're supposed to do!"

All the way home I am reviewing the whole harrowing incident when it suddenly hits me. What *was* it that Bootsie was supposed to do?

Bite *me,* maybe?

Jakey

Pets, wide-eyed children bring them home or beg parents for them and promise to take care of them. The parents relent, allow the beast in the door, and guess who ends up taking care of them? The mother. That's how I got stuck with Jakey, the cat from hell.

Jakey was a nervous, nasty, complaining and demanding cat. He ate like there was a famine in the land, and so fast that he'd throw up and then come back for more food. He managed to throw up on just about everything, including everything I treasured, like my piano. It wouldn't be so bad if he threw up on the top or on the fall board, but he threw up on the keys. That involved taking the piano apart and removing the keys to clean under them. He even threw up on my plants, plants that subsequently died. Walking barefooted in my household was out of the question. The vet said that he was perfectly normal, that some animals do throw up a lot because they are hyper. Hyper? One unexpected squeak and Jakey ended up on the chandelier.

Worst of all—to me, a musician—was his voice; a long, shrill, nerve-shattering trumpet blast that traveled around corners and tapped you on the shoulder. And he controlled me with that terrible sound because he caught on that I'd do *anything* and give him *anything* to shut him up.

Mornings were unbearable. He'd crawl along the bed right up to my sleeping form and shriek as loud as he could in my ear, then run like a neighborhood prankster who rings your doorbell and then runs and hides. I'd sit up in shock, and there would be no one there. I knew it was Jakey. He was my worst enemy in life. He was definitely out to 'get' me.

After four cat-ostrophic years, the unexpected happened. Jakey died. I was not happy that Jakey died, but I have to be honest with you. When the vet called and said, solemnly, "We lost Jakey last night," my sense of sadness was soon replaced by the thought of a normal Jakey-free life.

I went by the animal hospital to pay their exorbitant bill for two days of oxygen and aspirin, fully expecting that they would take care of the corpse, but they didn't. They handed me a receipt stamped 'paid in full' and an occupied body bag. Trouble is, it was August and about 95 degrees and I was on my way to tune a piano. I could not leave a dead cat in my car for several hours in such heat, so I was forced to rush home. I left Jakey with my son to set aside till the whole family could get together for a funeral service.

When I got home, the house was empty and I couldn't find Jakey anywhere. I couldn't imagine where he was. I looked everywhere. When my son came home, I asked, "What did you do with Jakey?" He answered in such a sweet, innocent way, as children do when they have done something they don't realize is horrific, "It was so hot, Mom, that I put him in the freezer."

I almost fainted. The thought of a dead cat in my freezer up against all the good food in there turned my stomach and made my head spin. I was too weak to handle the situation before I had a good night's sleep.

The next morning my son came to my bedside and said, "Mom, I know how much you loved Jakey . . ." where on earth did he get THAT idea? ". . . so I got up early and buried him right outside the kitchen window so he could be near you forever and you could see him every time you washed dishes . . . "

It couldn't be true! I jumped out of bed and rushed to the kitchen window and peered out onto a mammoth rock that said "JAKEY" in large white letters. My body went limp as I fell into an arm chair.

My son further consoled me with, ". . . and don't worry, Mom, his name will never wash away. I wrote it in bathroom caulking."

Blacky

It was already dark when I arrived home and found the note on my door: "We are sorry to have to tell you that your black cat was killed by a car in front of our house. You will find him by our curb."

With my pocket flashlight, I could see that they had placed his body on a wooden slab and adorned his head with flowers. Very thoughtful neighbors, but it didn't ease the blow of the tragedy. I wondered how Blacky got out in the first place?

My son came home to the bad news and together we wrapped the body for burial and found a suitable coffin. We dreaded breaking the news to my daughter, after all, it was really her cat.

She took it pretty hard and cried before, during, and after our mini-funeral service that was held out back by the light of the silvery moon.

After the last bit of dirt was thrown on the grave, we trudged slowly back to the house single file, heads and shoulders bent, crushed by the blow of our pet's untimely death. We needed to be together, to talk and share treasured moments with each other.

"He was so good."

"The best cat ever."

"Yeah."

"Remember the way he used to hide in paper bags?"

"And nap in the bathroom sink?"

"And the way he hung on the screen door in a perfect X."

"He loved to enter the shower stall and swat the water."

"I'm going to miss him a lot."

When there were no more tears left, we sat in silent misery, preoccupied with our own memories. Our painfully sweet reveries were suddenly interrupted by an eerie scratching at the back door.

We looked at each other in total bewilderment. Had Blacky's ghost returned to say goodbye? We huddled together and slowly and cautiously opened the door with our six eyes fixed at the base of it.

Blacky strutted past us with disdain at having been accidentally locked out, and headed straight to his dish. After chomping noisily on dry food, he curled up in his bed and went to sleep; this, as we three watched with open-mouthed disbelief.

Once we were certain that it was Blacky and not his ghost, we three had the same simultaneous startling realization: Who on earth is buried out back?

The next day we put an Ad in the paper: "Would the owner of a Missing black cat please come forward and claim your cat. We will exhume at your convenience."

Man, Dog's Best Friend

I went with my boss, George, to bring Polly, his huge black Neapolitan Mastiff, to the vet. You needed two people to do this; one to clear the way and one to pull the dog. The whole experience was something you might see in a Charlie Chaplain movie.

First of all, George kept an old car just for her, because her toenails were deadly daggers that could tear the inside of a good car to shreds in one minute flat. I ran ahead to open the door to the 1985 Bomb. Naturally, Polly is suspicious and refuses to budge, just like a donkey and about the same size only fatter.

I'm standing by the car door watching an over-6 ft George pulling with all his might on a leash wrapped around a thick neck that supported a head the size of three bowling balls. Polly would move – unwillingly – an inch at a time, so it took a very long time to reach the car. Naturally, she refuses to get in, so George is forced to turn into a crane and lift her. He's tugging and pulling, and she's squirming and wiggling. It looked like they're dancing a rumba.

He finally succeeds in raising the upper half into the car, then swings around back and pushes the whole rear end in, falling halfway into the car right along with Polly. Once she is in, the whole back end of the car sags.

So now we're driving along with Polly's head hanging over the front seat, and she's snorting and drooling over the two of us. George thinks this is wonderful. He's proud of everything about Polly, even her slobber. Meanwhile I'm trying to keep from throwing up.

We get to the vet and I have to run ahead to clear the waiting room out. The assistants move all dogs into another room so Polly could pass. However, it takes a very long time to get her inside, because now Polly knows for sure where she's going, and resists even more.

I looked out the door and watched George as he tugged and pulled Polly all the way up the path. He looked like he'd been beaten and mugged, with his tie flapping in the breeze and his glasses hanging from one ear.

George must be used to this struggle, because instead of going straight into the examining room to get it over with, he decides to weigh Polly on a rectangular floor scale in the waiting room. I wondered what made him think that Polly would agree to being weighed when she hadn't agreed to one single thing thus far.

Each time George pulled Polly onto the scale, she resisted with such a fancy tap dance, that the rubber mat on the scale was caught in her talon and goes sailing across the waiting room. After that, all you could hear is Polly's nails tapping and clicking against the metal top of the scale, sounding like someone is shaking a tin can full of thumbtacks.

Undaunted, George continued pulling her onto the scale. By the time he got the lower half on the scale, the upper half was off. After about ten tries, George thinks he has succeeded and says, "149 lbs." But, of course, he didn't notice that her hind legs were still on the floor, so that's only her partial weight. That dog has got to be 200 lbs.

As soon as we entered the examining room, the doctor came in, and to my surprise, he wasn't even as big as Polly. I couldn't begin to fathom an examination between a 150 lb doctor and a 200 lb dog. It was obvious that she couldn't be lifted onto the examining table, so he had to examine her on the floor. Even with George holding Polly with all his might, as soon as the vet touched her face to examine her inflamed eye, Polly lunged at him with George on her back. It reminded me of Captain Ahab in Moby Dick, being dragged into the sea on the back of the big White Whale. I shut my eyes and thought, "Oh boy, that's the end of the vet."

Everyone stood absolutely still so that Polly could calm down. I was so mortified at what the poor doctor was going through, that I shouted, "George, why must you have such a big dog? Is it the beast in you that is attracted to the beast in Polly?" But words are wasted on George. He is positively addlepated when it comes to Polly so that no matter what you say, he answers, "Isn't she wonderful?" No, George, she's not. She's a big, slobbering, clumsy hulk with sagging jowls that pull the lower eyelids down so that the red eye tissue shows, making her look like a bleary-eyed sot. Of course, you can think this, but it's a waste of breath to say it to a man who adores this monstrous beast.

The doctor finally succeeds in giving Polly a shot in the rear end and she's so thick-skinned, I don't think she even felt it. As we passed through the waiting room, the people huddled with their dogs at the far end of the room, looking terrified until we were out of the door.

They say that a dog is man's best friend. In this case, I think it's the reverse, because a dog this size has no other friends but a master like George.

The Day I Took Lola Out
or
Why, God, Why?

My Dear Daughter,
   The next time you shop for anything living, you might want to check on its breed and temperament. You had a Teacup Chihuahua and wanted a companion for it. I can understand that. The sellers handed you a tiny puppy that fit in your palm and they assured you would be the same size as ChiChi. Good Heavens, girl, you bought a Jack Russell Terrier that not only grew three times the size of ChiChi, but is so hyperactive that ChiChi is always hiding from her. Some companion! I am doing my best to watch her for you, but no human being, least of all me, has the kind of energy you need to handle this dog.
   Someone told me that caging for short periods helps a dog to settle down, so I tried that. When I let her out an hour and a half hour later, she had calmed way down. In fact, she was so good I decided to take her with me on my errands to two banks and a pet store.
   Well . . . . the minute she hit the car, she turned back into the pre-caged Lola, The Terror . . . I mean, Terrier.
   When we stepped into my car, I fixed a nice place for her next to me on the passenger seat, but she wasn't having any. She *insisted* on being on my left arm, like she was a two-pound ChiChi, only she's *not*

a two-pound ChiChi. She's weighs a ton. Try to drive with one dead arm, and that's the arm I needed to reach for the bank tube. The teller was laughing her head off as she watched me scuffle with Lola to get the tube. I didn't think it was so funny.

Every time I put Lola in the passenger seat, she did the Australian Crawl over my body to get back to the window. When the tube made that loud suction sound, it so frightened her that she tore across my body, clawing my boobs and hurling herself onto the passenger seat like there was an enemy attack. The minute it got quiet, she tore back over my body to the window again. Then she repeated the whole procedure when the tube returned, and you know how *that* sounds—like a gun shot. I was so haggard from restraining Lola that when the teller asked, "Would you care for a doggy bone?" I answered, "Yeah, and one for the dog, too." She sent two.

Lola snatched the doggy bone out of my hand and dove down to my feet. She was so hyper, she chewed it like a lion that just bagged a deer. Actually, that's how she handled *everything.* I couldn't drive with her blocking the gas pedal and the person behind me was getting antsy. Twice, I went through this, twice – at two banks. My poor boobs!

Then we went to the Pet store. She absolutely refused to stay in the car and refused to walk on the ground. I had to carry her in like a huge salami and I prayed there would be no other dogs in the store. I could hardly handle one. Two was out of the question.

Inside the store, I put her down and she grabbed hold of my leg and hung onto it for dear life. She wouldn't let go and I tried to walk with this ball and chain on my leg. I walked like I had one peg leg, so I had to pick up that salami again to go get two cans of dog food. She got me so rattled that when I went to ring up the stuff, I put her on the counter and said, "Now be a good kitty." The saleswoman looked at me, I looked at Lola, Lola looked at the saleswoman. We were all dumbfounded. See what happens when you have a dog that makes you crazy.

It didn't end. I forgot I had to mail a letter. There was no getting out of the car without her diving out after me, so I drove around to the drive-up mailbox. Again, she wouldn't let me mail the letter. We wrestled at the wheel until I heard an impatient beep. The woman behind me had been waiting ten minutes to mail her stupid letter, so I had to unhook my seat belt and do a right arm hammer lock on Lola's head, get the letter in the box, hook up my seat belt again, and take off—all this with Lola breaking free and jumping up and down and tearing back and forth across my chest; ouch, my poor chest.

When we got home, I was trying to get my pocketbook and small bag and open the car door. Lola flew into my arms like I was going to abandon her – which, incidentally, appealed to me by that time. Three curlers fell out of my hair with all of this wrestling, but she wouldn't let me pick them up. I couldn't, anyway, not having a third arm.

It is easier to carry two full bags of groceries plus a pocketbook than one Lola and a small bag with 2 cans of dog food in it.

Somehow I survived, sort of. You can tell that by the fact that I am writing this letter.

By the way, when are you picking Lola up?

Love (maybe),
Mom

The Ungrateful Frog

I was sitting at my computer when I saw something move on the floor to my left. I thought it must be a mouse. It wasn't. It was a frog, a tiny little grayish green frog. Now, where on earth did this frog come from? How did he get in my house? I didn't hear a knock. He must have found the key I lost out back.

The last time I saw a frog here, it was on my bed. Now *that* was a *real* shocker! I called my daughter and all she could say was, "Why don't you kiss it? Maybe it'll turn into a prince." It didn't work last time, so I wasn't going to kiss *this* one. I'm not stupid!

I could have stepped on the frog, I suppose, but I didn't want to stain the rug, so I had to think of a way to capture it. Without a plan in my head, I went into the kitchen. I figured there might be something there that would trigger an idea. I saw a small, square bag and a fly swatter. I had no idea what I was going to do with either one, but I picked them up.

When I came back to the computer, the frog was gone. I looked and looked, and I finally saw him. He was traveling south, migrating toward the bathroom. Maybe he had to go. I leaned forward and pushed open the bathroom door, and the little frog jumped right in. A very accommodating froggy!

I followed him, but he was so fast, I lost him again. Then I saw him in a corner, facing the white tiled wall like he'd done something bad and was self-punishing. All he needed was a dunce cap. So I put

125

the bag in front of him and planned to make a distur-
bance with the fly swatter to scare him into the bag,
but guess what? I didn't have to. The stupid frog
jumped right in the bag, like he wanted to get out of
there. I closed the top of the bag so he couldn't jump
out—not that he tried—and carried him to the deck,
and set him free.

This may have seemed a charitable thing to
do, but with the raccoons, the possums, the wood-
chucks, the coyotes, the squirrels, the bears, the deer
and the birds, he was facing a string of land mines
from the house to the pond. Well, I reasoned, he
made it to the house from the pond, maybe he'll get
lucky again and make it back to the pond.

I've never had another frog since then. He must
have made it back and then spread lies about me so
no other frog would make the trip.

What an ungrateful frog!

POLITICAL

The Two Votes

I

The phone rang just as I was about to leave for work one gloomy overcast Tuesday. It was Ruth, my civic-minded neighbor, calling to tell me that *this* was the day.

"What day?" I asked with mild concern.

"What do you mean 'What day'?" she mimicked. "Haven't you seen the banners in the center of town?"

"I use the back roads."

"You must have gotten the circulars in the mail," she continued.

"I throw junk mail out."

"Don't tell me you haven't heard the PA announcements blasting through the streets?"

"Ruth. Just tell me." I glanced at the clock. If I left now, I would be right on time for my piano tuning job.

She gave an exasperated sigh and answered, "It's Board of Education Election Day."

"Is that all?"

My lack of interest triggered her political zeal. "Don't you realize how important this is?"

I shrugged my shoulder, concerned only with the time.

"Do you know what would happen if the wrong people got in?" she threatened.

"Things would probably improve," I answered, cynically.

"You know that isn't true."

She wasn't getting anywhere with me, so she paused for a moment, then switched tactics. In a softer tone, she asked "Aren't you friends with our candidate's wife?"

"I do know Beth, but we never discuss these things."

"Everyone knows that her husband is a decent human being who fights for the underdog."

"I know, I know," I answered.

"And you certainly know that Winegoe gave up time from his law practice to save the two old trees in the center of town."

"Hurry up, Ruth, I'm late for work."

"These are dedicated people who are concerned about our town and our children. We need people like this on our Board of Education. If we have any civic conscience at all, we've got to do our best to get them elected."

"I can't talk any longer, Ruth, I have to go."

"O.k., but remember, if every concerned person got two other people to vote, we'd have it made."

"Look, I can only promise that *I'll* vote, but I don't see how I can get others to vote. I'll be tied up all day, and I really know nothing about the issues. If I tell someone to vote and they ask me a question, I wouldn't know what to tell them."

"Just keep in mind that if the other people get in, our school system will go down the drain. They don't even have children in the school system. All they want is power and control. They don't care about our children."

"Ruth, I have to go. Old Lady McGill is waiting for me and I'm twenty minutes late already. Look, I'll try, but I've got to run, now."

As soon as we hung up, I turned on the answering machine, reached for my toolbox and flew out the front door with Ruth's final words still ringing in my ears, "Don't forget! Two votes!"

II

Old Lady McGill was watching for me and had her front door open before I even stepped out of my car.

"Steps slippery," she cackled, "Hang onto the railing."

It had long since stopped raining and the steps were practically dry, but to appease a 92-year-old woman, I held onto the railing.

The front door led directly into the living room. The drapes were drawn and it was dark except for a dim floor lamp in the far left corner of the room. I stepped inside and by the time my eyes adjusted to the dark, Ms. McGill had made her way to the far right side next to the stairs. "Piano's over here," she called.

I walked gingerly across the living room, feeling my way around marble-top tables and a velvet parlor set and stood next to her. The piano was a huge dark mass against the wall at the foot of the stairs.

"You need more light?"

"Yes, I do."

"WHAT?" she shouted.

"YES!" I answered loudly.

"She shuffled over to the dim floor lamp, unplugged it, and dragged it across the living room in total darkness.

Once the lamp was set up, I could see that the dark mass had corners and a keyboard, but it was still too dark. Rather than make demands on a nonagenarian in a room in which the draperies had not seen the light of day for half a century, I resorted to my flashlight and began the examination.

She came up behind me softly, pointed upwards and said, "Bathroom's at the top of the stairs," followed by, "Do you need papers?"

"No, thank you." I continued checking out the piano.

"What?"

"No!"

"WHAT?"

"I. . .DON'T. . .NEED. . .PAPERS!"

When she placed the papers under me, I got the distinct impression that she thought I wasn't toilet trained.

I thanked her for the papers nonetheless and continued examining her piano. It was in bad shape.

"Wires look good," she said. I didn't know what she was talking about.

"What wires?" I asked.

"WHATCHA SAY?"

I cupped my hands over my mouth and bellowed, "WHAT. . .WIRES?"

She pointed to the strings.

"Yes," I nodded, approvingly. I could see they were rusted, but at least they weren't broken in such an old piano.

No sooner was my head back inside the piano when she asked, "Is it very out-of-tune?"

"Yes," I answered in a normal voice, preoccupied with the examination.

"WHATCHASAY?"

I pulled my head out of the piano, leaned toward her and shouted, "YES. . .OUT. . .OF. . .TUNE,"

She thought about that, then said, "S'funny, it was tuned when my mother bought it."

That had to be at least eighty years ago, but what's the point in telling her now at age 92 that a piano should be tuned no less than once a year?

After a few more ear-piercing conversations, I was actually permitted to work. Ms. McGill kept inspecting periodically, but after a while, I was so engrossed in restoring this old piano, I didn't even hear her anymore. A few hours later, she startled me with, "Would you like a cup of tea?"

With tool in mid-air, I gently refused. "No thank you, I'm only halfway through this job and I have to pick up my children at three."

"WHATCHA SAY?"

The tool dropped out of my hand and down into the piano. In total exasperation, I answered as clearly as I could, "NO. . .NO TEA!" then I proceeded to open up the bottom of the piano to retrieve my tool.

Fifteen minutes later she returned and cheerfully announced, "Your tea is ready. Come into the dining room, please."

It was no use. I put down my tool and with a feeling of utter hopelessness, joined her at the table. She had fixed a neat little tray for me complete with bone china and antique silverware. Nothing for herself. The thought of "Arsenic and Old Lace" passed through my mind, and I examined the tea carefully before and after each small sip.

For lack of anything better to say, I asked, "DID. . .YOU. . .VOTE. . .TODAY?"

"Yes, I already had my lunch. I don't take tea now until two."

I took a deep breath and began again. "DID. . .YOU. . .VOTE?"

"VOTE? Didja say 'VOTE'? Vote fer what?"

"BOARD. . .OF. . .EDUCATION," I mouthed loudly. "GINSLER. . .AND. . .WINEGOE. THEY ARE THE..." and here, I thought of the old Westerns, "THE *GOOD GUYS*."

She thought about that for a while, focused her faded blue eyes on me and asked, "And who are the bad guys?"

"SOME LADY. . .AND SOME MAN," I shouted. I didn't want to confuse her with names and I'm not certain I KNEW the right names.

"A lady, huh?" But your two are the GOOD guys?"

"I nodded."

She hobbled over to the massive carved desk between the two windows and rummaged through the clutter. In a Houdini sweep, she pulled out a circular and held it up to me. "These the ones?"

I nodded.

"You're sure they're the good guys, now?"

"Yes," I nodded.

I finished my tea and returned to the piano. I heard her dialing the phone on the desk. She spoke so loudly, I could hear every word.

"Hello, Maude, couldja do me a favor? WHATCHASAY? Couldja drive me over to the Middle School? The lady here says I hafta vote. The good people are. . .lemmee see. . ." She fumbled for the circular but could not find it this time. "It's. . .I think it's JIN-SLER and WINE-O. They're the good people. That's right. Three-thirty. You sure that's all right? Many thanks, Maude."

With continuous interruptions, I did not finish the piano by three and since I was booked solid the rest of the week, I was forced to return later, after tending to my children.

III

After dinner and a trip to the polls, I returned to Old Lady McGill's house. We went through the slippery stairs routine once more, even though the stairs were completely dry now. I held onto the railing once more. I guess she must have developed a little faith in my bladder, because the papers were gone.

When I finished the piano, she offered me tea. Once again I refused and once again she made the tea. I noticed immediately that she had not only given me my used tea bag, but my used napkin turned inside out as well. Since I wasn't poisoned in the afternoon, I figured it was safe to have another cup of tea with her.

After the tea routine, I asked, "DID. . .YOU . . .VOTE?"

"Of course," she answered, but you know, I almost made a mistake. The two good people were not together on the board and I almost voted for the top two. Good thing I brought my spectacles."

After tea, she paid me and saw me to the door. I turned to her and patted her gently on the back, "THANK. . .YOU. . .FOR. . .VOTING."

"WHATCHASAY?"

"GOOD. . .NIGHT!" I shouted.

"Goodnight," she answered.

She stood in the doorway and waved until I was out-of-sight.

IV

Exhausted, I dropped deep into my favorite armchair with a sigh of relief. Suddenly, I bolted forward. The second vote! I forgot all about the second vote! It was late and there was only one more hour to go. What was I going to do? I promised Ruth.

My friend, Pat, came to mind. She'd never do it, I thought. She hates kids and couldn't care less about the Board Of Education. In fact, if all the schools in town vanished, she would consider it an answer to prayer. But what choice did I have? It was too late to do anything else.

I dialed her number and could not think of one single argument to get her to the polls, so I said, "Pat, I want you to go over to Middle School and vote for Ginsler and Winegoe. Why? Because if you don't, I'll never speak to you again."

She did, and my mission was accomplished.

The Council Meeting

It is a hot and humid summer evening and the Borough Clerk has forgotten to turn on the air conditioning in the council room. The Lady Mayor enters, followed by the six Councilmen, most of whom are antagonistic toward their first female Mayor. After a little whispering, throat-clearing, and paper shuffling, they settled into their seats on the dais and the meeting is ready to begin.

The Lady Mayor conducts the usual opening formalities: a flag salute and a moment of silence. She then makes an unscheduled announcement.

LADY MAYOR: A matter has been brought to my attention that needs immediate resolution, so I will put it before you first. There is a dead bird on the border of our town, and the Board of Health in both towns do not know which town has the legal obligation to dispose of it. Residents from both towns are gathering in the area, so it must be resolved immediately to avoid a border dispute.

COUNCILMAN 1: I got the notice in my box about this bird at 6:45 this evening, Mayor. You never let us know in advance about anything and then expect us to make decisions on matters we haven't had a chance to examine. (With that, he shoves his papers away from him in disgust and falls back angrily in his seat.)

COUNCILMAN 2: This is nothing new. We're always the last to know anything. Maybe we don't need a council, just a mayor. (Under his breath he mutters, "She does what she wants anyway.")

COUNCILMAN 3: Just a moment! I was there when the call came in and. . .

COUNCILMAN 2: We know, we know. You're the knight in shining armor, always around when the mayor needs you.

LADY MAYOR: Councilmen, I got the call about this matter at 6:20 tonight. How much sooner could I possibly have gotten the notice in your boxes?

(Here, three angry councilmen talk at once in a sort of verbal mutiny against the Lady Mayor, and are silenced by the mayor's pounding gavel.)

COUNCILMAN 4: Which way is the bird's tail pointing?

LADY MAYOR: What is the relevance?

COUNCILMAN 4: Maybe the two towns can agree that whichever town the tail is pointing to has the responsibility of getting rid of it.

COUNCILMAN 5: That's ridiculous! (He frowns and turns his head in disgust.)

COUNCILMAN 6: It can't work. What if the body is on our side and just the tail is on theirs?

MAYOR: We're not playing games here. This is a serious matter and we need a fair and equitable solution that will best serve the residents of both towns. Perhaps our Borough Attorney has a suggestion.

BOROUGH ATTORNEY: There IS a Statute on the books that pertains to animals on the street that have been killed by motor vehicles. Do we know whether a moving vehicle killed this bird or whether it died of natural causes? To research the exact law, I must know how the bird died.

LADY MAYOR: We don't have time here to order an autopsy. The dispute is attracting spectators from both towns and needs to be resolved now before there is violence in the streets. Borough Clerk, please make a note of the results of our Borough Attorney's research in the event of similar future happenings.

BOROUGH CLERK: Will do. (He touches his pencil to his lips and writes in his yellow legal pad.)

LADY MAYOR: We open the floor to the public for suggestions.

(A tall elderly man with wild white hair and furrowed brow stands and speaks in a loud, oratorical voice.)

MAN: This is another example of the abominable way in which this administration handles things! It was the same way with the leaky roof matter, and I sit here wondering whether I'm going to have rain on my head. . .

LADY MAYOR: Sir, it's not raining. Do you have any suggestions concerning the bird issue?

MAN: . . .and what I find appalling is the money charged for the Engineer's bill that almost slipped through. . .except for an oversight. . .

LADY MAYOR: Is that all, Sir?

MAN: . . .except for an oversight. . .

LADY MAYOR: Thank you, Sir. Anyone else?

(Suddenly the council room door bursts open and a breathless woman rushes in and stands before the Mayor and Council.)

WOMAN: Mayor, I'm the one who called you and I thought you should know that a cat has come along and has run off with the bird.

(This message sends a wave of murmuring and foot shuffling across the dais. When it subsides, a councilman with a serious, pensive look on his face speaks up.)

COUNCILMAN 4:   Was the cat licensed?

My Theory of Re-election

Council Meetings in my old town were unusually long because of the constant bickering with their first female Mayor. They resented her and fought her bitterly on every issue, causing the meetings to drag on and on to five hours. Most council members can hold out for three hours, maybe even four, but by the fifth hour—that fatal fifth hour—each one becomes who he really is. As a result of attending these excruciating five-hour meetings, I have formulated a Theory of Reelection that I believe to be foolproof. My conclusions are based on personal observation of these councilmen.

Councilman 1, by the fifth hour, has folded each finger over the next, towards the thumb so that his hands look like giant lobster claws.

Rule: Never reelect a person who changes species at a meeting. He's a lost claws.

Councilman 2 is the Invisible Man. By the fifth hour, he does not seem to realize that he's still at a public meeting and that there are people present. With unblinking staring fish-eyes, he stands up, walks around the dais to stretch his legs, and with a series of tiny tugs and fancy footwork, extricates his impacted shorts, this, followed by spasmodic adjusting.

Rule: Never reelect a man who thinks he's invisible. You never know what ordinance or resolution he may extricate or adjust because he thinks no one can see him. (You might want to put him on the Board of Adjustment.)

Councilman 3 nods to everything, like that clown head that you might see suctioned onto a dashboard.
Rule: Never reelect a council candidate whose neck is on a spring. He's good for nodding.

Rule for Councilman 4: Never reelect a man who acts in the first hour like it's the fifth. He is so disoriented, there is a whole separate meeting going on in his head. He continues to argue points that are not being discussed. For example, his mind is fixed on the problem of geese flying over the rec field leaving slippery droppings that the players may slip on, while the rest of the councilmen are discussing the Salary Ordinance.

Rule for Councilman 5: You can, however, reelect the person who acts in the fifth hour like it's the first. He is the mortar for the rest of the bricks.

And as for Councilman 6, he represents the greatest rule of all: Always reelect the person who falls asleep by the third hour. He's the only sensible one up there.

The Building Inspector

As a single parent of two, I was all set to advertise for boarders for the remodeled rec room area of my split level house when there was a knock at my door. Standing there was a pudgy pink-faced man who opened with, "I'm the Building Inspector."

I was flattered that so important a person would come to welcome me in my new home, and was very cordial to him. But he was stern, and asked, gruffly, "What have you done to the garage door?"

"You can plainly see that I've removed the overhead door and installed a regular door. You can't expect future roomers to be raising and lowering an overhead door, can you?"

"You can't do that."

"I can't do what?"

"You can't just alter the garage doors."

"Why not, it's my house."

"Well, you need a permit when you make changes."

"You mean, you need a permit just to change from one kind of door to another?"

"Yes."

"And I suppose you also need a permit to put a makeshift kitchen in the back of the garage?"

He gasped.

"Follow me. I'll show you," and I led him through the new rental area and opened the door to the back of the garage and showed him where I partitioned it off to put in a basic kitchen. No sink, just a stove and cabinets for the roomers. If they need a sink, they could use the one in the shared bathroom.

The Building Inspector stood there looking pre-cardiac arrest, with bulging eyes locked on the cute little stove I had installed. I thought for sure that he would compliment me on my ingenuity, but he didn't. His face was crimson and his heart must have been palpitating, because his head developed a noticeable tremor in time to his heartbeat. He stayed like that for so long, I was getting worried. Was he going to cry, or was he going to die?

"Don't tell me this is not allowed, either," I asked.

Visibly shaken, he mumbled something about the gas pipe along the floor and the fire code, so I said, "If I knew you were going to take it so hard, I wouldn't have done it. Do you want me to tear it out? It's OK if you do. I'll just take it out."

He didn't answer right away, as though in deep thought. After he calmed down and took a few deep breaths, he said, "Look, tell your roomers that they can make a cup of coffee on that stove, but they can't roast a chicken."

"Fine, I'll tell them that," and I showed him out.

About six months later, I got a call from this same Building Inspector and I asked, "What did I do now?"

"Nothing," he said, "I was just wondering if you had a room to rent. My wife and I are splitting up and I need a room right away.

So he came over and I showed him the rear room that had just become vacant. Then I opened the door to the makeshift kitchen and I said to him, "You can have the room, but there's one thing I have to tell you. You can make a cup of coffee on that stove, but you can't roast a chicken."

The Political Conference

Out of curiosity, I went to an Annual Conference of the New Jersey League of Municipalities in Atlantic City. In case you don't know what that is, it's a once-a-year opportunity for municipal officials from the 567 New Jersey Municipalities to get together for four days at taxpayers' expense to share ideas and programs. They attend seminars and workshops on current issues affecting municipal government; and, in a few cases, get to know their secretaries better.

The sinus problem in the next room sent off a series of fog horn blasts that were my 7 AM wake up call. The seagulls must have mistaken it for a mating call, because with that blast, they would fly in from all directions, fighting for first place on the ledge outside that window and spilling over onto mine. Each morning I'd shoo away the squawking birds so I could enjoy the magnificent view. The early morning gray sky blended with the gray ocean mist in the distance, circling back to ripples of white surf against the sandy beach below my hotel window.

The first morning, I had a slight problem registering. I didn't know they were going to ask for a municipal title to type on my badge. Since I held no official position, I choked out "Mayor's Attendant." I wore the badge proudly until I learned that people thought I was a mayor's personal valet who shined his shoes and brought him coffee. I didn't like that very much, so I went back to registration.

It's a good thing there were different workers at different tables that issued badges. It enabled me to register again with someone else. I gave them a new title, "Municipal Attendant." This time people thought I handed out towels in a municipal building ladies room, so I went back a third time. This time I got it right. I was now "Administrative Assistant." That solved the problem because no one, including me, knew exactly what that meant. People didn't want to show their ignorance by asking, and I certainly didn't want to show my ignorance by answering. It sounded impressive and genuine and I was treated with more respect and dignity.

These four days expanded my vocabulary. I learned what a government expert is. He's the guy from out-of-town who shows slides. And tipping is not what it sounds like. It's the fee paid by the municipalities for garbage disposal. And the new term for treated sewage is "biosolids," which can lead to new municipal swearing: "Oh biosolids!" And organizations, they are endless. There's NJAFEWO—women in government; and PETE—plastic recycling; and NJRPA—recs. and parks; and VALIC and JIF—insurance; and ABC—Alcoholic Beverage Control. Unless you know all of these letters, it's hard to understand municipality conversations. At first, I thought they were speaking in highly classified code.

Women mayors gravitated toward each other. They had similar problems. They agreed that because of male bias, they had to be twice as competent to gain half the esteem, and that men resented taking orders from a woman. Some men overcome it with a light dalliance.

A married official and his paramour, the female tax assessor, were at the conference, but I never saw them. Nobody did. They never came out of their room. He did not know that I knew about their affair. (After the conference was over, I ran into him at the municipal building, and with a wide-eyed innocent look, I said, "I saw you at the conference and took such a wonderful picture of you and your wife!" I still laugh when I remember the look on his face. Talk about a deer in the headlights! I meant to, but never got around to telling him that I don't even have a camera.)

From five o'clock on, after the daily classes were over, the weary officials who actually *did* go to classes, attended lavish receptions given by large corporations. These were corporations that either already deal with municipalities, or who would like to deal with municipalities, and no amount of expense was spared to gain the favor of municipalities. Through them, food and liquor flowed like Niagara Falls. I remember looking into one of these reception rooms and seeing a pyramid of shrimp that practically reached the ceiling.

My last night at the conference I was at one of these receptions. The crowd had thinned as many had already gone home. My body was weary from four days of walking and talking. I was sitting alone at a small table with my head in my hands and resting my tired feet on a chair. I had a rare splitting headache. A man came over and introduced himself as the owner of a pharmaceutical company. Bleary eyed, I looked up and said, "You're just the one I want to see. Have you got an aspirin?"

"No," he said, "but I have condoms." In my exhausted condition, I thought he said condos, so I said, "I would love to have one of those."

When I finally caught the gist of what this man was really saying, one of the lady mayors happened to wander over. I pointed to the man and said to her, "This gentleman here has condoms. Are you interested?"

With that, the man turned on his heels and literally ran from the room like he was being chased by a pack of rottweilers.

Still staring in the direction of the man's speedy exit, the lady mayor said, with feigned philosophical wisdom, "Isn't it reassuring to know that old lechers are practicing safe sex?"

Our sides were splitting with laughter all the way to the final Dessert Reception.

MUSIC

He Never Dropped a Beat

One day I heard that a great jazz pianist named Vernon would be coming to town. There were rumors that he had been on the road with Duke Ellington, but it was not unusual for jazz musicians to exaggerate. Maybe they would sit in with a top band, and the next thing you knew, they are telling the world that they were on the road with that famous band for ten years. It didn't matter to me because this guy was such a great jazz pianist, I didn't care what he said. I just wanted to hear him.

It's not a good idea for a woman to go to a jazz club alone, and this night, all of the musicians I knew had gigs, so I ended up bringing a non-musician escort. I hate going to hear music with non-musicians. They do not have the love of jazz and always start talking. There could be a great creative idea being played, and a non-musician will desecrate it by talking all through it.

My friend, Herbie, a bass player, made the mistake of bringing his date to a jazz club to hear a great jazz bassist. He became so irritated over her constant chattering through the music that he slapped a wad of bills in her hand and sent her home in a cab so he could listen to the music. Only another musician could understand this.

Entering that club was like stepping into a sepia cavern of thick smoke and clinking glasses and bustling waiters and wall-to-wall finger popping jazz enthusiasts. There was such excitement and energy radiating from the bandstand that no one noticed two white people joining them. We were totally immersed in this powerful music when a young, beautiful woman in a form-fitting silver lamé dress rose from her seat near the bandstand. As Vernon played, she stepped over to him, put her arms around him lovingly and planted a kiss on the back of his neck, then turned and looked smugly at the other women in the room. This was to let them all know that she was his 'Old Lady.' Once she oozed that message to the crowd, she sat back down.

Watching this scene from the rear of the club was an equally attractive, shapely woman who had arrived a few minutes earlier and witnessed this touching scene. No one noticed that as she made her way slowly through the crowd toward the bandstand, she had picked up a beer bottle, gripping the neck of it in her hand and hiding it by her side. She came up behind Vernon, raised the bottle high in the air and brought it down on his head with great force, spraying the bandstand and nearby tables with shards of glass. The music continued, but a chilling silence swept through the room as the stunned audience waited for the next move.

Not content to see the blood trickling down Vernon's neck over the spot where his paramour had kissed him, she leaned over to give him a verbal blast even more penetrating than the blow. You could hear her fury above the music. "You jive-ass motha f—a . . . You ain't fooled me . . . Ah knowed about you and dat . . ." As she was delivering her scathing tirade, Vernon rose slowly from the piano bench in his unruffled cool, arched his right hand into a fist, and while comping on the piano with his left hand, turned his torso slightly to the right and delivered a perfect uppercut, then slowly sat back down and continued comping with both hands.

With the delivery of that perfectly placed punch, her body rose above the people, then dropped down and disappeared from sight. Almost immediately, the heads began swinging in time to the music and finger popping began again. In five minutes, she was history. She must have been dragged away, because we never saw her again. We never saw the silver lady again, either. She probably slipped out through the kitchen when she saw the wife coming, IF that was the wife. Who knows? And what was my tone deaf friend's assessment of the whole scene? Sheer admiration. "What a guy!" he said, "He never dropped a beat."

Lucky

One night I played a duo with a drummer at a club called The Embers, a miniature replica of the Embers jazz club in New York. It was owned and run by a most unlikely aging couple. The wife would sit at the back of the club and knit, which was somehow inconsistent with the nightclub ambience. She belonged in a rocker on the porch of the Little House on the Prairie.

The owners had a boxer named Lucky who had the run of the club, obviously ignoring health codes. Unfortunately, his favorite spot was under the spinet piano, to the right of my feet, where people couldn't see him. I don't know what they fed this dog, but in the middle of the most beautiful and romantic tunes, there would be a wave of the most foul stench wafting upward from Lucky that rendered everyone around him unlucky. In street vernacular, it would be classified as silent but deadly. It may well be in the category of what destroyed Sodom & Gomorrah.

A friend of mine entered the club and walked over to say hello. I had no way of warning him, and he stepped into the danger zone. He opened his mouth to speak, and gagged. With a vacant look on his face like he'd been clubbed and was about to fall over, he backed away. Instead of a hello, it was more like an "aarrgghhh." During every break, I'd join him at the musicians' table and say, "That dog! That dog!" and he'd say, "Oh, stop trying to blame the dog."

Midway through the gig, between the foul odor and the accusing glances of people passing the bandstand, I was developing a splitting headache. Finally, I couldn't take it any longer and I did something unprofessional that I never ever did before or since. I got up from the piano, walked straight to the door, burst out of there and started running as fast as I could toward my studio. Forty feet behind me was Peter, this high school jazz enthusiast who showed up at all my gigs, and forty feet behind him was my friend who came to hear me play. So here we were running down the street toward my studio like a disconnected caravan fleeing from a band of marauders. When I reached my studio, I shut my door on the two of them and opened a back window to draw in some fresh air and to cool my burning face.

An hour later, the phone rang. It was the drummer. "What happened? You left me up there holding my drum sticks. We looked all over for you."

"You looked all over for me? Where would you look, Hal?"

"We looked behind the club, and stop calling me Hal."

"Why would you look behind the club? What's back there?"

"We all figured that you and those two guys were so overcome with passion, you all went behind the club to make out."

"In the middle of a tune?"

This mentality shows that creativity is no respecter of intelligence.

The next day, I was telling the musician who rec-ommended Hal what happened the night before. Then I added, "Why was this drummer so annoyed when I called him Hal?"

"Because his name is George."

"George? Why does everyone call him Hal?"

"Oh, we call him that behind his back. It's short for halitosis."

No wonder I ran out of the club. Between the dog and the drummer, I didn't stand a chance.

MISCELLANEOUS STORIES

My First Plane Ride

It was an exciting day in my life. A relative in Florida was getting married and it would mark my first flight in an airplane. The whole day was spent in joyful preparation for the trip; packing and looking forward with great expectation to this new experience.

Only when I found myself at the airport looking up at this huge metal bird did it hit me that my feet would no longer be safely on the ground. It's one thing to think about a plane ride and another thing to be right there. I had second thoughts about entrusting my life to that mechanical contraption and tried to think of excuses not to board. But alas, it was too late. They already had my luggage and people were pushing me along.

The first thing I noticed inside the plane was that it wasn't full. Was there something others knew about this plane that they weren't telling me? And the second thing was, when I boarded the plane, it was light out, and the minute I got to my window seat, it was dark out. This certainly had to be a bad omen.

I sat stiffly in my seat, wanting desperately to get off, but it was too late. The stewardess was telling us over the PA system to fasten our seat belts. As the plane taxied to the runway, I felt faint. How was I ever going to get through this?

The next thing I knew, we were going straight up. I was in agony. The lights below got smaller and smaller and I couldn't look anymore. My eyes were tightly shut and my seatbelt was still on when I heard the stewardess say, "Would you care for a drink?" She could see the state I was in.

Without thinking, I answered, "YES!!" But then when she asked me what I would like, I couldn't think of the name of a drink, because I don't drink. Then I remembered that there was a drink that tasted like plain orange juice, and I knew I could probably get that down, but I had a hard time remembering the name. It took several tries before I could say "Screwdriver!!"

It was an eternity before she returned with my drink. I paid her quickly and the instant her back was turned, I chugged it down in two gulps like a veteran drinker and waited for oblivion. I felt a warmth spread from my throat to my chest, and I was becoming so very relaxed. I wondered why I never drank before. It's not so bad, I thought. It makes you feel pretty good. I should have done this long ago.

I unbuckled my seat belt, looked straight down at the tiny lights, and said, "I'm not afraid of you," and I sat way back in the seat, ready to enjoy the trip. And why not? I was pleasantly high.

No sooner was I totally relaxed, comfortable, and unafraid, the stewardess came over to me, leaned over and said, "I'm sorry, Miss, I forgot to put the vodka in your drink."

You Can't Go Home Again

A guy from the high school group that I used to walk to class with called after many years. I expected a scintillating report of his life since our group parted at graduation, or at least a nostalgic reminscence of the fun we had back then. But it turned out to be the most painfully boring conversation I have ever had in my entire life.

How does a person get so boring? I figure there must be an over-the-counter Boring Pill, and this guy took a few before calling. Talking to him was like buying a ticket to a play and finding it so abysmally boring that you want your money back. After his call, I wanted my brain back.

When he called, I was sick in bed with a fever, sore throat and an ear infection, so I did not have the energy to resist his onslaught of negative tales. He went on . . . and on . . . until I was in a stupor, near comatose, trying to repress a death rattle that was rising in my throat.

First, I had to hear about his mother's dementia, the unabridged version.

Next, his marriages. The first wife died of throat cancer. The second one died of breast cancer. Then there was his prostate cancer, and without so much as a breath in between, he careened right into the cancer and death of his good friend, another classmate. What I got out of listening to him was that he's a very dangerous person. Everyone around him develops cancer and dies. I hoped it couldn't be transmitted over the phone.

Every time I thought his talking would end, he would embark on another chapter, like his family. His daughter's fiance of 15-years vanished just before the wedding, and there were the ongoing fights with his son who never married nor left home.

I didn't think his self-centered siloloquy could get any worse, but I was wrong. Most excruciating of the whole saga was the detailed account of his career as a fifth grade teacher. He described thirty-two years of pre-teen classroom misbehavior as well as behind-the-scenes teacher infighting. It was here that I think I found out what was wrong with him. He spent so many years in the fifth grade, he's still there. I think I hate this guy.

It still wasn't the end. It seemed like there would be no end until one of us died during the conversation. He went on to complain about his pension, his health coverage, and today's cost of living. My eyes rolled way back in my head and I let out an audible groan. He thought it was Emily, my cat. Actually, I think he knew it was me, but since all his prior listeners were dead, he was desperately in need of a new audience, and he wasn't going to let me go.

Between the high fever, the strong medicine, and the unbearable boredom, I began fading in and out. I think it's called 'hallucinating.' I don't know how long he talked or what he was saying when I caught a few condescending words about religion or religious people. He caught himself, stopped, then said "You aren't religious by any chance, are you?"

I sensed an opportunity here and answered in a soft, raspy voice, "Yes, I am."

You never saw a person end a conversation so fast in your life. It was like I shone a light in a condemned building and all the rats scattered.

I resolved in that moment that if I *ever* see this guy's name on my caller ID again, so help me, I'll have whoever is around answer the phone and say, "She's dead. Don't call anymore."

And if he asks when I died, they will be instructed to say, "Just after your last phonecall."

It's a Bird, It's a Plane, It's . . . a Plane

Here is a letter that I wrote on a flight to Boston. I had flown only once before, so it was like the first time all over again. It didn't help that I was given a copy of The Boston Strangler to read on the plane.

Dear Jeanne,
 Here I am on board a plane. I'm shaking so hard, I can hardly write. And we haven't even taken off, yet! The last time I felt this way, I was in a dentist chair.
 Why do I torture myself by sitting near a window? I'll tell you why. This window is near an exit and I feel safer near the exit. What kind of irrational thinking is that? What good is an exit door in mid-air? I must be going mad.
 The stewardess just gave me two aspirins. The propellers have started up. I feel sick. In two minutes I'm going to give her back the two aspirins—liquid form.
 Now the plane is moving. I think I'm going to faint. I tried to distract myself by taking a picture out the window. It's such a bright, sunny day. I was so nervous, I used a flashbulb.
 We're on the runway. Now we're going up-up-up. Just look at the pollution! What are those dots? My goodness, they're cars. They look like ants.
 Gee! The plane just tipped waaay to the right and now, waaay to the left. Can't this pilot make up his mind? Might have to use the little bag.

Took some pictures; I already told you that.

This is nice, great; now take me home.

More turning. Doesn't this pilot know the way? Are we circling the airport? I don't know if I can bear an hour of this. Once in a while the plane flutters. Why does it flutter? Are we going to rip in two? It's so scary.

Here I'm afraid to look out a 5-storey building and I have my eyes out this window looking straight down. If I believed what I see, I'd die here and now. But this window is like a TV set. I'm just watching a picture, so I don't see it as real.

Now we're higher. I don't see anything but clouds below me.

The wing that I thought was broken seems to have straightened out. Must be a panel that flaps when the plane is on the ground, but straightens out in the air. Why is the plane shaking? What does that mean?

I can't continue writing. I'm too panicky. I have to go into a self-induced coma till we get there. If we don't meet again, Jeanne, you've been a good friend. Goodbye.

Why is the plane shaking? It shook me back to the present. I think we're going down. My ears! We're going through clouds. Still in the clouds, but my heart is already on the ground. I'm shaking all over again. My fingers are sticking together. I think my tongue is swollen. What was that bump? Where are we?

A big flap on the wing has come out. The stewardess has told us to fasten our seat belt. I didn't have to. I never unfastened it.

There are drops on my window. Is it raining out? I think I see land. We're landing! My ears! What an ungodly roar! What was that? Did we hit something?

We made it! We're on the ground. We're stopping.

Flying is pretty neat, Jeanne. Not bad at all.

A piece of cake, actually.

See you next week.

Your friend,
Lucille

Homemade Standup Comedy

Humor is like the air, it's all around us. And it's the silly things that happen that change your whole mood and outlook.

When my toaster broke down, my good friend bought me a new one. I don't know where she got it, but it belongs in a Charlie Chaplin movie. When the toast is done, you hear a gunshot, then the toast goes flying through the air. So my day begins with catching flying toast. It is so ridiculous that I can't help laughing every morning. My friend unwittingly gave me more than just a toaster.

Then there's that cat from hell that was left with me for two weeks, but stayed sixteen years. She took possession of my favorite chair and wouldn't let anyone sit in it, not even me. Whenever I said, "Go to your room!" she'd jump on that chair. It was her territory. If a guest innocently sat in that chair, this cat would climb up on them and give them no peace until they moved, then she'd curl up on the chair smiling victoriously. The sight of a grown person standing there glaring indignantly at a mere eight-pound cat after being ousted from a chair has me howling.

One time I had to call the IRS with a question. Would you believe that the background music while on hold was *The Nutcracker Suite*? Is it possible

that someone at the IRS has a sense of humor? It reminded me of the time I played a Brain Surgeon's party. We started the gig with the old standard, *"You Go To My Head."*

We live in a melting pot where it seems that every other person has an accent. I had lunch one day in a group with an assortment of accents. One man was extolling the virtues of the ex-President with, "President Butch, hees tried to bring 'piss' throughout the world." I choked on my food on that one. The other person said, "I not so crazy for Boosh." I just kept nodding to everything and kept eating for fear that if I stopped, I would burst out laughing, and I didn't want to be rude.

Then there's the time I saw a reflection of my black cat on the kitchen table (not the 'chair' cat above) and rushed into kitchen with a rolled up newspaper and swatted the cat. It turned out to be my black pocketbook. Can you imagine how stupid I felt standing there with a weapon in my hand threatening my pocketbook?

There is very little room for humor in the area of medicine, so it is usually unplanned. Like when I asked the doctor what is causing that noise in my head. He looked up from my file and said, "That's the sound of your arteries hardening," then looked

172

back down in the file. I never found out if he was serious or not.

Another time I asked this same doctor, "So what happens when a person has a heart problem? They just go on until the heart stops?"

He said, "Well . . . ya gotta die of *something.*"

I had a problem with my right shoulder once, so I went to the physical therapist. I burst out laughing when he said, "Just pull your shoulders up into your ears." I don't think he realized how funny that sounded . . . nor how difficult it was to do.

Then, there was the dentist who was looking deep into my mouth, looking and studying, then he says, "Your arm-pits itch, don't they?" I was astonished that he was able to see all the way down to my arm pits through an open mouth. As it turned out, I had a mild case of Lichen Planus, a condition that affects your gums and makes your armpits itch. Who knew?

My friend, Joan, is a nurse who works for a gyne- cologist. They have a routine that is as precise as a trapeze act. She prepares the patient for examina- tion. When the doctor enters, as he is greeting the patient, she rolls his stool in a certain spot so the doctor can sit and examine the patient. It's like clockwork. Well, one day the doctor came in, greeted the patient who was on the examining table with her legs in the air, then he sat down—only the stool wasn't there. Joan had a lot on her mind and forgot to roll the stool over. The doctor ended up falling on his back on the floor. Joan stood over him, crying, "Oh no, Dr. Cho," and from the floor, he's saying, "S'awright, Choannie, s'awright." The patient, her view blocked by the sheet across her elevated legs like a white wall, cannot see what's going on, hears the crash and is screaming, "What happened? What happened?" All at once, the patient is screaming, the nurse is screaming, and the doctor is screaming and trying to reassure everyone. It is definitely a Saturday Night Live potential. I could see Carol Burnett as the nurse.

I see where that little boy in England fell into a gorilla pit. How gentle those massive, primitive beasts were! They all gathered around his unconscious body and looked at him quizzically. One even touched him gently. And then it happened. He woke up, took one look at these hairy beasts standing around him, and let out such a scream that the whole family of gorillas ran for their lives. I know just how they felt. I would do the same thing if I heard a scream like that; run, and keep running, like Forrest Gump. Those little mouths are lethal. Ever hear them in restaurants? That sound would scare anything. When they said on the news, "The boy is in the hospital and doing very well," I expected them to continue with, "but all the gorillas are dead from shock."

And nothing is funnier than bloopers. I just read an Ad by a man looking for an old beat-up tractor. He wrote: *Is your tractor an eye soar? I will cart it away and your clean yard will put a smill on your face.*

As I said before, Humor is like the air. It's all around us, so take it all in and let it put a smill on your face.

Dan Tang Chiffon
or
You Just Bought Yogurt

I was puzzling over the receipt that I had from grocery shopping. It was so peculiar, I wondered if perhaps the supermarket hadn't given me a secret military code by mistake.

This is what it said (my comments added):

HOMO GAL – Did I really buy one?

IDAHO POT – But Your Honor, I didn't even KNOW Idaho grew pot.

SAND BAGS – Is there a flood coming, by any chance?

AUNT MILLIE – That's all it said, so all I could think was, thank you, but no thank you. I already have an aunt.

SPIG SPAG – I kinda liked this one. It sounds like the name of a 1920's Charleston tune, "Spig, Spag, Varsity Drag!"

Frt Trp – WHAT on EARTH is this? It sounds like what you do after you eat something that doesn't agree with you.

Esca Sp – You gotta be kidding. I have plenty of Esca Sps, whatever THAT is.

Cant Bel Btr – Can't WHAT? If at first you don't succeed . . .

Of course, there were many more listings:

SS SHD/WHEAT – I understand WHEAT.

SCHW 2LTR DT – Isn't that the shakes you get from drinking?

APP R/D MED – Reads like a doctor's prescription. Or maybe you need a doctor's prescription after eating it.

BER ML OL OL – Is this an ethnic OL OL dance?

GU WH ASP SP – This CAN'T be edible. It's POISON SNAKE!

And finally, MOT CN/AP SC – Translation: If you eat any of the above, you're a dead man.

Any resemblance between this list and the actual food that I bought is pure speculation – except for the Shredded Wheat. THAT, I understood.

The supermarket needs either an archaeological linguist at the exit door who has experience deciphering writing on cave walls, therefore can translate the above for the customers; or they might provide a therapist for the persistent customers who go batty trying to decipher the list for themselves.

Maybe just a better writer would do.

(Dis)Order In The Court

I accompanied my part time boss, George, to a municipal court to try a case. We put two hours in the parking meter, then went up to the second floor courtroom. It was an unusual courtroom, different from any I had ever seen. While the dais was the standard oak, the room was set up like an amphitheatre with actual theater seats with wrought iron sides on the aisle seats, and the room was double the size of any other municipal courtroom I have ever been in. Could this room have once been a theatre?

People were lined up outside the prosecutor's office at the rear of the courtroom to give their explanations and, hopefully, get their charges downgraded. After this, they would only need to appear before the judge for a minute or so, pay their reduced fine, then rush back to work.

My boss and his client went to the prosecutor's line while I walked down the aisle to the front to listen to the ongoing trial. It had to do with a tree that had a dead branch hanging over the next door neighbor's property, a branch that was no longer in existence. Mr. Pro Se was strutting back and forth from the table to the zoning official, who was on the witness stand, asking questions in the dramatic manner as if he were a famous criminal lawyer arguing a high-profile murder case. He was in his 40s but was dressed like a 1960's hippy, with faded jeans and unbuttoned wrinkled shirt. In his right hand he carried a huge Sherlock Holmes magnifying glass that he used on the thick yellow pad of notes in his left hand.

Noting that the courtroom was filling up with settled cases that needed discharging, the judge asked, "Mr. Pro Se, how many more pages do you have to go?"

"Only two more, your honor." What he failed to say was that each page represented over an hour of questions.

After the first two hours, it became apparent that Mr. Pro Se was crazy, and from time to time you could hear sounds of disgust and impatience traveling like electricity throughout the courtroom. The people were anxious to pay their fines and get out of there, but Mr. Pro Se ignored every admonition of the judge, and every restless sound of the annoyed audience, and went on his pedantic way, like he was F. Lee Bailey.

I had to run outside and put another hour on the meter, so we were now entering the third hour of Mr. Pro Se's Dead Branch Saga. The room was very warm and stuffy. The judge's eyes were rolling back in his head, and he shut them from time to time to escape to a better place. And the Prosecutor was so weary from screaming, "I object," that he waved a resigned hand toward Mr. Pro Se as if to say, "What's the use, it won't stop him." Then he fell into a peculiar laughter, sort of like the glee of the insane.

The zoning official had been sitting so long, he was stuck to the oak witness stand and Mr. Pro Se's questions were becoming more and more bizarre, such as, "What kind of car were you driving when you inspected the tree?" He was stopped repeatedly by the judge with, "Mr. Pro Se, we've already answered that three times," or "We covered that at the last trial." If Mr. Pro Se heard the judge or the prosecutor, he didn't let on but simply kept going on and on, relentlessly, until everyone in the courtroom was horizontal.

After two and a half hours, it was obvious that there was no end in sight, so the judge bolted upright and announced, "We're gonna hafta call a recess so I can get rid of the rest of the cases in the room."

The instant those magic words were uttered, the courtroom was filled with spontaneous applause. Normally, if you so much as whisper in a courtroom, you open yourself up to the judge's admonition, "We'll have none of that in MY courtroom!" In this case, the judge was so beaten down with exhaustion, he allowed the people their outburst. He must have figured that after two-and-a-half-hours of this unbearable case, they were entitled.

The applause was still going on as George stood before the judge. Referring to the applause, the judge said, "Is that for you, George?" and George answered, "No, your honor, it's for you." They both appeared outwardly serious, but the corners of their mouths turned up slightly, almost imperceptibly, revealing the humor of the moment.

Our case was over in minutes, so we went downstairs to the first floor cashier so our client could pay his reduced fine. All of the cases in the courtroom were resolved quickly and the people lined up behind us, still agitated from being held hostage for two and a half hours in what had to be one of the most excruciatingly boring trials in the History of Law.

The people who lined up at the cashier's window represented a cross-section of society, but at that moment, all differences vanished. There was no race, no gender, no age. We were simply a group of human beings united in the agony of an unbearable experience that we shared and probably will never forget. Had we been aboard ship, we would definitely have banded together in either a mutiny or jumped overboard en masse.

There was such relief among the exhausted, overheated people, many held their heads and groaned, "Oh my god, I can't believe it's over. I thought we'd never get out of there."

Others were a little more specific and vented the following remarks:

"They shoulda tied him to that dead tree."

"Tied him? They shoulda hanged him from it."

"I betcha if someone shot the guy, the judge woulda thanked him."

"I was getting ready to take up a collection and pay the damn fine to shut the guy up!"

"How would you like to live next door to that guy?"

"How would you like to be MARRIED to that jackass?"

And on and on.

I was so dehydrated when we left the sweltering courthouse that my tongue stuck to the roof of my mouth. I had George stop so I could get an ice cream soda. He got an ice cream cone. Watching a man change from a powerful criminal lawyer who had just saved a man from losing his license and who got the jail time dropped, into an overgrown kid licking an ice cream cone, gave me an idea. Maybe that's the solution. If a case gets too overbearing, call a recess and pass out ice cream cones. Can adversaries be angry if they're sitting around licking ice cream cones together? Then again, maybe this idea was a symptom of my own delirium caused by two-and-a-half hours of courtroom sense-deprivation.

No Green Thumb Here

Once upon a time, I lived in a town that gave awards to residents and businesses that maintained, improved, and beautified their properties. Out of curiosity, I attended one of their ceremonies and every person who was called forward, regardless of age or stage received a plaque and an individual congratulation and handshake by the Mayor. They beamed with pride, and I was jealous. I wanted to go right home and beautify my land so I could have an award, too.

After that, I received a brochure from a plant company and on the cover was a picture of the most beautiful roses I had ever seen. I stared at the perfect flowers and thought, why can't I have that on my property? I sent for them and then forgot all about it.

One day a box arrived. I didn't recognize the return address, but I tore it open with great curiosity. It contained gnarly black things that I think I've seen on Twilight Zone or Outer Limits. They looked like evil creatures that were dropped by UFOs into the black lagoon where they reproduced, then retrieved and sent out to select homes to hypnotize and capture earth people. My name was obviously on their list.

I was so afraid of the contents that I threw the box toward the back door. Then, in sheer terror, I pushed open the door and shoved the box out with a broomstick and locked the door behind it. I avoided going in the backyard after that.

A few days later, a friend came by and said, "What are those rose bushes doing strewn about out back?"

"Rose bushes?" I looked out the back door. "Those are rose bushes?" In my ignorance, I thought the plant company was going to send me rose bushes that looked like the picture. I didn't know they would send gnarly roots that needed to be put in the ground.

Not that I didn't trust my friend, but I just couldn't touch these ominous-looking things, so she planted all six of them. Once out-of-sight underground, I was able to take care of them. They were just beginning to come up when along came Dudley, my son's dog. He lifted his leg on every plant, and in time, stunted their growth and they all died. I was not happy to lose these bushes on my very first attempt at gardening. I didn't speak to Dudley for a long time after that.

Then one day a friend of mine gave me an amaryllis plant. Despite my tragic experience with the rose bushes, I was still harboring a secret desire to grow something, anything. So I took the fuzzy bulb and stuck it in potting soil as she directed. I kept the pot on my counter where I could nurture it.

In no time at all, bright green blades shot out of the rich soil and grew, it seemed, a few inches a day. I was deliriously happy. In the center of these blades, a rigid shoot appeared with what looked like praying hands on the end. When it was two feet high the praying hands split into two pods. Then each pod split into two more pods. I started to feel like a veteran gardener.

As these pods began to open, a pink fringe peeked through and I could hardly contain my joy. One morning, at the height of my enthusiasm, I awoke, entered the kitchen, and found the pods lying on the floor. I was gravely distressed. What could have happened? They were doing so well.

It turned out that my cats were jealous of my attention to the plant, and they slapped the pods right out of existence. The stalk stood there in the middle of the plant like a headless giraffe, waiting to die. It did, and with it, my interest in gardening.

So my hat's off to those stalwart gardeners with their bright green thumbs who can win the battle over pets, insects, and weather conditions, and go on to win their well-deserved prize. As for me, my lot is to thumb through gardening catalogs and enjoy the pictures.

Thanksgiving

In my search for a heartwarming Thanksgiving Day story for a publication, I started interviewing people. I was expecting joyful tales of family reunions with long lost uncles and cousins and nieces and nephew; but alas, I couldn't find any. Apparently, behind the façade of smiling faces around the dinner table on Thanksgiving, there lurks a whole silent undercurrent of family annoyances, people having to go where they don't want to go, seeing relatives they don't want to see, complaints about bratty kids, having to hear the same stories over and over by grandparents, etc. It was shocking! Here's what a few said.

One woman carried on a long soliloquy when I asked her if she was looking forward to Thanksgiving. She said, "I dread Thanksgiving! Every year we *have* to go to my daughter's house or she gets mad. But she cooks like she drives. The last time I rode with her, she was complaining about some tickets she got for moving violations, and while she is telling me about it, the car is moving along but her head is turned towards me. So I ask her, 'Who's driving the car? You're not watching the road!' She reacts strongly and indignantly, 'Whataya `mean?' While she is fighting to defend her driving, she takes her eyes off the road again. The car goes over a curb and comes to a stop on a field. The only trouble is, it is a church graveyard and we are parked on some-one's grave. Her cooking is the same. She believes her Thanksgiving dinner is perfect, but you bite into the turkey and it bleeds. Every year I get closer to shouting 'For goodness-sakes, cook the damn turkey longer!' but I don't want to make trouble. I try to keep peace in the family; meanwhile she is turning us all into vampires."

In another case, when I asked where they were going for Thanksgiving, they said, "To Uncle Pete's." Then she goes on to say, "Uncle Pete, Oh my god, Uncle Pete. Wonderful cook, but he grew up in poverty and has kept very peculiar ways despite his rise out of poverty. His wife used to be a carefree, generous person, but over the years, she turned into him. Putting up with one of him is bad enough, but two of him is more than anyone can bear."

"Part of Uncle Pete's pathology is that he is compelled to organize people's refrigerators. When he visits family, he barely says hello at the door, but walks past everyone and heads straight to the refrigerator. He's got to make sure that everything is arranged in the proper sequence, taller items in the back and smaller ones in the front. And the butter has to be where the butter belongs, and the milk has to be where the milk belongs. No matter how much organizing the family does in anticipation of his visit, he always finds something that's out of order and lets them know it."

"Thanksgiving Dinner at his house is both a blessing and a curse; a blessing because he is such a good cook, and a curse because of his peculiar ways. He doesn't like waste, so you must only put as much as you can eat in your plate. There cannot be any leftovers or he carries on. He sits at the end of the table toward the kitchen so that all plates are checked by him on their way to the dishwasher. Whatever is left in the relatives' plates is scooped onto his plate and he devours it, even if it's two peas and a carrot slice. He cannot tolerate wasting food, so that part is the curse. He is very proud of the fact that there is no garbage in his house. How could there be, with a human disposal like him around?"

Let's just pretend that I didn't get to interview a "normal" household this year; maybe next year. Until then, I wish you all a Happy Thanksgiving.

BATHROOM HUMOR

The Valentine Present

She was 30, beautiful, sparkling grey eyes, and a crown of bright red hair. You'd spot her in a crowd immediately. After finishing college and launching a medical equipment sales business, she was ready to settle down. She finally found Mr. IT, and talked endlessly about the new man in her life. "He's wonderful! Has an important job with a dental firm! We really hit it off. He's very attentive and calls me all the time!" and on and on.

I supposed that this meant that I wouldn't be hearing from her very much. With such an overwhelming fixation, she'll probably never play piano again, therefore, there will be no reason to call me to tune her piano. If she doesn't call me, how would I ever know the rest of the story? This is one of the setbacks in Tuning. You have to wait six months to a year before hearing how things turn out.

Her call surprised me; after all, it had only been six months since the last tuning. Is she back at the piano? What happened to Mr. IT? After tuning her white Kimball grand, she told me the sad tale over a cup of tea.

She had only known Mr. IT for a short time, and savored every moment with him. Valentine's Day was coming up, and he had a surprise for her. He invited her to an early dinner, then they would take a trip to High Point to see the magnificent view of three states, and there, he would give her a Valentine gift. However, she made an unfortunate mistake. She had a bowl of pea soup at dinner, forgetting what pea soup does to her.

The plan was for her to follow him in her car to the peak of the mountain so they wouldn't have to go out of their way back to the restaurant to get her car. After the drive to the top, they walked to the tourist area to enjoy each other's company and take in the romantic view.

After many warm embraces, he gave her the most beautiful gold heart-shaped pendant that had garnets and tiny diamond chips bordering it. She showed me. It was lovely.

But something happened. The pea soup started to act up. It kept churning and growling in her stomach and she began experiencing excruciating pains. Such intestinal activity put a pall over this romantic tryst. She tried to ignore it, but the pains became so intense, she had to find a way to get out of there and get some relief.

He locked her in his arms and they kissed passionately. She then tore herself away from his embrace and made a hasty beeline to her car where she immediately remedied her problem with a major explosion. Deeply relieved, she opened her window to wave goodbye to her paramour, put her key in the ignition, and was about to take off. She did not see that Mr. IT, still on his romantic cloud, impulsively ran toward her car.

To her utter horror, he stuck his head in her window for a final farewell kiss, then stopped short, as though he hit an invisible barrier, which he actually did. She says that his eyes began to spin in opposite directions and his hair parted down the middle. He withdrew his head slowly, carefully, like a drunken turtle, took a few deep breaths, and whispered hoarsely, "I'll call you," and staggered back to his car.

He never called again.

A Very Ghastly Husband

I've been running into the same woman in the dentist's waiting room several weeks in a row, and we've become sort of friendly. I noticed that she was particularly glum this day, so I said to her, "Don't tell me there's someone more afraid of the dentist than I?"

She answered, 'Oh, it's not that." She lowered her eyes, "I'm getting a divorce.'"

I could see she wanted to talk. I was willing to listen—anything to get my mind off the dentist.

She began, "When I married him 15 years ago, he was so wonderful, so alive. I felt I had someone to lean on and we were completely happy for six months. Then every night he began to yawn and yawn and fart and fart and belch and belch. There was no end to it. I was never brought up to do such things without excusing myself. I tried to bring up the subject with him as delicately as I could, and his answer was an angry "If I had to run to the bathroom every time I had to fart, I might as well sleep in the bathroom!" Frustrating as the situation was for her, I had all to do to keep from bursting out laughing.

She continued. "I suppose I should have been more sympathetic," she said, with deep regret in her voice, "but the disillusionment after only six months of marriage was more than I could bear. We began growing apart from the start."

I was very little help to her in her dilemma. I figured that if every woman complained about the sounds that emanate from their husband's orifices, there would be very few marriages left. It was hard to keep a serious expression on my face while she described life with her noisy mate.

Trying very hard to be compassionate, yet seeing the underlying humor in the situation, I asked "Are you trying to tell me that there was sort of a green cloud hanging over your bed all these years?" I couldn't hold back my amusement any longer and began to giggle.

She started to smile, but then became glum again and continued, "It wasn't the smell so much that disturbed me. It was the horrible sounds that burst out of both ends simultaneously, punctuated by screaming yawns, even throughout our most intimate moments."

I lost it after that and said, "You mean . . . you felt that you were continually facing a firing squad?" She caught the humor and we both burst out laughing and it took us a while to calm down.

"It got worse and worse," she continued, "and he began to see me as the enemy. So whenever I tried to approach him for a little affection, he would spitefully conjure up ammunition and fire at me. He apparently was able to do this at will."

I told her that a skunk does the very same thing when an enemy approaches. The thought of this made us convulse with laughter. I had to put my head in my hands. We made such a racket, the dentist must have wondered what was going on in his waiting room.

She said, "I put up with it for years until I just could not stand it any longer. He even did it in his sleep and it would wake me up all the time. I couldn't go on like this. I walked around sleep-deprived for years. Finally, I had to have my own bedroom so I could get a full night's sleep, so I moved into another bedroom. We have had separate bedrooms for several years, now . . ." or did she say "seven years?" Whatever. I can't remember. ". . . and the latest is that he has become resentful, not only to me, but even to our friends. If I invite people over, he won't join us. He invariably sits in his room next to the living room spitefully emitting these loud and sometimes long, drawn out expulsions, to everyone's embarrassment. It has made me so disturbed that I am seeing a psychiatrist."

The poor psychiatrist! He has to listen to this with a straight face. It wouldn't be professional for him to burst out laughing at an earnest and tearful patient. Granted, this was no laughing matter, but this plot, if not the lead article in a Psychiatry For Today magazine, would have been a booming hit comedy on Broadway. (No pun intended)

I found it amazing that this woman would open up so freely to me, a complete stranger, but she was so burdened that she had to tell *someone.* How could an educated, well-dressed woman whose husband had a responsible position with a big New York firm, admit to such humiliation with family or friends, or even with those who have already been to her living room?

Every time I think of her husband, I can't help laughing. Why didn't he try to save the marriage? He might have tried including her in his extra-marital activity by saying "Pull my finger" so she could feel that she was at the controls; or by feeding her beans three times a day so that she could add harmony to his melodies.

If he were enterprising, he would have taken up baritone sax and joined a band; that way he could let out all those low notes – sometimes with the horn and sometimes without – and get paid for it. Or perhaps he could have a side job at a lighthouse during a storm or fog, standing out on the tower firing warnings to boats to keep them from crashing on the rocks.

What I'm really curious about is, what does a woman say to the judge at the divorce hearing? "Your Honor, my husband is ghastly"?

And what can the judge say to that? He probably does the same thing himself to some degree — although perhaps not to the First Degree like this husband.

And is there a name for her grounds, like Extreme Nasal Cruelty? Or maybe A-BAM-donment? How about Ir-rectum-cilable Differences?

There I go again. I can't stop laughing.

Her Movie Debut

According to the news, there is a flu epidemic in this area. Everybody is sick right now including Joan, one of my close friends. She called me up today and sounded terrible. She said, "My husband and son both have brought home colds, so naturally, I caught one, too. The trouble is, I'm sicker than the two of them put together. I'm the only one who ended up going to the doctor. He gave me some antibiotics and I've been trying to drink a lot of liquids.

"Last night, my fever was down a little, but I was very congested and couldn't sleep. I was restless and I didn't want to wake my husband, so I put on a heavy robe and went downstairs. I took the antibiotic, stretched out on the couch, and put the television on. You wouldn't believe what happened."

I wondered what could possibly happen at midnight in her living room.

She said, "There was this movie on. It was about an earthquake in New York City and eight people were trapped in a collapsed subway tunnel and they were trying to find a way out. Every exit was filled with debris, so the whole movie had to do with their underground quest to find a way out.

"There were all kinds of obstacles that this group had to overcome on their search for freedom. At one point they decided to go under the East River and walk to Brooklyn because there simply was no way out in New York. The way seemed hopeless.

Joan took a sip of orange juice, and said, "You know, antibiotics don't agree with me. It gives me such gas and it makes me feel so bloated and uncomfortable. I never could handle the stuff."

Returning to the movie, she said, "These eight people went under the East River and naturally, there was water seepage, just enough to create fear and tension. Next thing you know, they are either swimming, or pulling themselves through the rushing water by hanging onto a pipe. Well, after a few tense moments, they end up out of the water and are walking through a tunnel looking for another exit.

"At that point, I had such a terrible gas pain from the antibiotics, I couldn't hold back, and I fired a loud expulsion that sounded like BeeeeeeeeWop! Good thing I came downstairs or I would have awakened the whole family. I couldn't believe what followed.

"Instantly, the group in the movie stopped and everything got quiet. Then one guy said, 'What was that?'

"Frightened, another one whispered,'I don't know.'

"Suddenly, they all screamed, 'It's GAS!!' and they ran for cover in eight directions, taking shelter behind anything they could find in the tunnel.

"The timing was so perfect," Joan continued, "I thought they all heard me. I was even embarrassed. Then I started to laugh, and I've been laughing ever since. A moment like that happens only once in a lifetime."

I told her, "Joan, just think of it as your movie debut, your first bit part, only the word isn't 'part.'"